ANDRÉ BRETON TODAY

ANDRÉ BRETON TODAY

Edited by

Anna Balakian and Rudolf E. Kuenzli

WILLIS LOCKER & OWENS • NEW YORK

Printed in the United States of America

Published by Willis Locker & Owens
71 Thompson Street, New York, NY 10012

Library of Congress Cataloging-in-Publication Data

Main entry under title:

André Breton today.

  Bibliography: p.
  1. Breton, André, 1896–1966 – Criticism and inter-
pretation. I. Balakian, Anna Elizabeth, 1915–
II. Kuenzli, Rudolf E.
PQ2605.R35Z576 1989   841'.912   89-2482
ISBN 0-930279-16-6
ISBN 0-930279-15-8 (pbk)

COVER: Man Ray, *André Breton*, c. 1930. Collection Lucien Treillard, Paris.

CONTENTS

Introduction

Anna Balakian

Viewed in its totality, the work of André Breton falls into three categories: the theoretical and philosophical essays, his narrative prose, and his poetry. The last two facets of his writing substantiate his modernism, which the first category announces. In a somewhat gothically constructed eighteenth-century prose, the theoretical texts belie automatism; they are sometimes a rebuttal to hypothetical abuses, personal and impersonal, creating a one-sided debate, expressing personal passion, critical, existential, and political, in a tone eloquent and didactic. Unlike Mallarmé's theoretical prose, which consists primarily of an *a posteriori* ars poetica composed after his major poems were written, Breton's are *a priori* for the most part and as such very deceptive, because they do not totally predict the direction his own creative powers were to take in their subsequent development.

More than twenty years after his death, however, it is the theories and postulations that have remained the major target of critical attention, and there have been tendencies to debunk them—an easy task because they constitute an area of vulnerability in their emphatic approach to dogma. In an extraordinary essay that should be reprinted, the late Robert Champigny pointed out meticulously but benignly the inconsistencies in Breton's use of the words "Surrealism," "reality," and "reason" by standards of normal logic, which Champigny found totally incompatible with surrealist discourse. His intelligent but inconclusive essay serves to demonstrate the confusion that arises when one tries to define Surrealism in accepted logical terms.[1]

Another area of Breton's expository writing that is not totally persuasive to commentators is the polemical and circumstantial. Breton acknowledged this pitfall himself in a letter to critic Léon Pierre-Quint, the editor of Sagittaire, which printed and reprinted so many of his works. In connection with the reprinting of the *Second Manifesto,* he wrote in 1945 that he had reservations about the violence of his 1930 polemics in view of the subsequent fate of some of the writers he had attacked, and not just Artaud and Desnos.[2]

Regardless of such flaws, these expository essays are great texts because they are brave and demonstrate a power of conviction that made of Breton an unusual person in that "age of anxiety" of the twenties and thir-

1

ties better known for its indecisions. They prove by way of their tone as well as their content what Marcel Duchamp called "Breton's catalytic power" in an interview I had with him shortly after Breton's death. As a result of the compulsive reader-response these writings generate, the manifestoes in particular, and lately some of the other essays, have received considerable coverage and have been translated into a number of languages, although regrettably the later collection, *La Clé des champs*, and the posthumously collected pieces, *Perspective cavalière*, remain largely unavailable and have not yet appeared in English. The translation of *Le Surréalisme et la peinture* has done much to bring Breton to the attention of art critics and historians. These essays have been quoted and challenged often by those who had no knowledge or sense of the whole context and circumstances of the corpus, nor of the motivations of a young man who, as he declared, had known what it was to stand at attention in the army and did not want to carry that routine into his personal life pattern.

These writings have succeeded in reinforcing the pontifical character of the portrait of Breton (will he ever outlive the label of "Pope of Surrealism"?); his theories have also perpetuated the notion that his basic contribution to literature is the promotion of automatic writing, that it is a total commitment and the basis of his entire work. There prevails also the narrow assumption that because he sought to interest Freud in the Surrealists' exploration of the unconscious, his orientation is totally Freudian in his attitudes toward the dream and toward sexuality. Thus his work is currently being subjected to psychocritical Lacanian interpretations and his nontheoretical work is being read in terms of "fear of castration" and sadism. There is on the contrary ample proof that Breton's knowledge of psychiatry predated Freudian extravaganzas and that indeed Freud was noncommittal about Breton's work when it was brought to his attention. In the current volume Mary Ann Caws refers to this exchange between Breton and Freud in her observations on *Les Vases communicants*.

On the other hand, Breton's narratives, consisting of *Poisson soluble, Nadja, Les Vases communicants, L'Amour fou,* and *Arcane 17,* have been with the exception of *Nadja* mostly neglected in scholarship. I call these works "analogical" as opposed to logical because, instead of following an organization conventionally appropriate for the philosophical or even biographical essay, they proceed on the basis of analogy between one thought couched in metaphor and another toward which it gravitates. It is surprising that they have not caught the attention and the expertise of those engaged in stylistic studies and in rhetoric. Michael Riffaterre looked at *Poisson soluble* stylistically,[3] but no one to my knowledge has broadly and comprehensively scrutinized the gravitations or magnetism of the metaphor in Breton's analogical prose. Instead, there has been a profusion of articles on *Nadja* in a rather repetitive way and in the context of the novel genre, a genre ironically rejected by Breton in his *First Manifesto*. Haim Finkelstein and I, working on the bibliography of Breton in 1973–74, found fifteen comprehensive commentaries on *Nadja* within a single decade but total neglect of the other two books of the trilogy. Renée Riese Hubert gives precise information about these Nadjas in her *"Nadja* depuis la mort de Breton."[4]

Interest has picked up in *Les Vases communicants,* which Breton considered his most interesting prose.[5] There is still nothing substantial about *L'Amour fou* although, recently translated by Caws, it is now more available to Anglo-American scholars; it has caught the attention of book reviewers and there may be an upsurge of commentaries to follow. Margaret Cohen's article in this collection of essays is an encouraging beginning. In one of the most important sections in *L'Amour fou* Breton demonstrates in his analysis of an early poem, "Tournesol," the essential approach to the analysis of his poetry in general. *L'Amour fou* also gives the most revealing clues both to Breton's character and to the process of creativity subjected to his autoanalytic procedure.

The most amazing lacuna in Breton criticism has been the virtual silence surrounding *Arcane 17* following Michel Beaujour's early and illuminating article which, as an afterword to the 1965 paperback, has served as an orientation to Breton's multilayered work.[6] A 1986 book by Pascaline Mourier-Casile, *André Breton explorateur de la Mère-Moire: trois lectures d' "Arcane 17," texte palimpseste,* is the most comprehensive and detailed commentary of the interweaving themes and emblems of this dense text.[7] This seminal prose of Breton shows more than any of the others how the process of analogy can incorporate mythopoesis into a form of psychoanalysis. Two very strong trends in current criticism could merge in numerous scholarly responses among those who are currently engaged in an upsurge of rereading the avant-garde.

I continue to consider the poetry the most important part of the Breton corpus, although Breton was very modest about his poetic writings. He did not even mention them in a form he filled out for Biography News Services: Who's News, in 1962.[8] He considered his poetry per se a lesser manifestation of his poetic act than his political pronouncements and his ideological writings, but authors are not necessarily the best judges of their works. Without hesitation I would posit that it is the poetry that makes Breton eligible for greatness, placing him in the lineage of the esoteric poets of Western civilization from Shakespeare to Blake, to Novalis, Hugo and Yeats. This poetic work beckons to literary critics for commentary on its structure and modus operandi. Stamos Metzidakis makes a move in that direction here in his essay on Breton's poetic originality as he probes Breton's propensities toward the primordial. To date, commentaries on the poetry have been primarily thematic: love, death, liberty, types of imagery, and a few insights into his lexicon. Detailed analyses

3

like those included in this collection – Ronnie Scharfman on "La Mort rose" and John Zuern on "La Maison d'Yves" – are few. The model for such analyses was set many years ago, but not much followed, by Judd Hubert's "André Breton et le paradis perdu."[9]

The main target of close analysis has been the *Ode à Charles Fourier,* probably because its references are tangible and Breton's attraction to Fourier explicable; but one comes away from these exhaustive studies with more knowledge about Fourier than about Breton. Michel Beaujour's essay in this volume points out a new direction. The fact that Breton tackled the epic genre and gave it a modern adaptation in this and in other post–World War II writings needs not only to be recognized but compared to the efforts of other modern poets engaged in this type of genre-mutation.

In responding to this dense, esoteric, erotic, semantically compact poetry one has to realize that its automatism is very partial, coming in spurts, that there is indeed dynamic variation in Breton's poetics, that his major poems belie many of his theoretical assumptions, and that there are affinities between Mallarmé and Breton in terms of structural premeditation and metaphoric progression in the construction of palimpsestic imagery in spite of the great differences in lifestyle and attitudes about life that have set them apart.[10]

Following Breton's autoanalysis of his reconstruction of "Tournesol" we discover that his perception of reality has three concurrent registers. First, there is the objectification of desire, which makes him identify with objects in his aleatory path and brings him into confrontation with passing human figures. The second register consists of hermetic messages found hidden in Paris landmarks of statues and fountains serving as semiotic emblems. These and other hermetic images can generally be decoded by close reading of Fulcanelli's *Les Demeures philosophales* or other gnostic source books. His "one in the other" analogies, of which one part has its reference base in hermeticism, as in the case of the layered meanings of "Tournesol," have not yet been explored in any extensive way. The third level lies in his analysis of his state of psychological motivation at each stage of his life. Most of the automatism of his early poetry involves references to this third and personal level, which in his analysis of "Tournesol" remains admittedly enigmatic even to himself.

When we come to his later poems, we find that they are much more structured, and the third and automatic level less innocent and more contrived. Michael Riffaterre has illustrated this structuring in relation to "Guerre" and *Fata Morgana* in an essay, "Intertextualité surréaliste."[11] In fact, *Fata Morgana* is perhaps the best example of a technique which gives the illusion of automatism but turns out to be tightly structured. It is a tapestry of interwoven referential systems, representing war, exile, recuperation, without having direct reference to circumstantial data. In the

4

absence of appreciable critical commentary on this major poem, it is appropriate to reveal here the response of Léon Pierre-Quint, his editor and prominent critic of his time, upon receipt of the poem on October 2, 1941: "*Fata Morgana* enchanted me; the poem has a rare gentleness and is perhaps the one where you express yourself the most completely. The rich and beautiful themes which succeed each other are impressive."[12]

And what of *Les États généraux*, the poem of cataclysm and revolution, written in New York in 1943? Silence on both sides of the Atlantic Ocean in regard to a spiritual landmark so pertinent to both sides and a tribute to modern man's struggle for liberty. As for his final prose poem, *Constellations*, it was difficult of access for academic study before Breton's death except in Gérard Legrand's exquisite but rare anthology of Breton, *Poésie et autre* (Gallimard, 1960). This extraordinary serial response to Miró's gouaches by the same name is now readily available in *Signe ascendant* (Gallimard), a paperback collection of his later poetry. This prose poem should invite much critical attention since it is most indicative of the structuring methodology of Breton, illustrating his definition of poetry according to other than rhetorical gauges. It reflects his ultimate commitment to a monistic philosophy embracing the artist's ecological and cosmic habitat. It is in this vision that the linkage between Breton and Octavio Paz, as well as many remarkable and neglected poets of Latin America, becomes manifest. The sociologist-philosopher Michel Maffesoli, a half-century younger than Breton and one of the few writers outside of the literary and art disciplines aware of Breton's work as well as that of Paz, has written two books on the functioning of the human imagination in its responses to the activities of the cosmos. He concludes with his observation of what he calls "transcendent immanence":[13] "The precarious and the aleatory are in step with the irresistible continuation of things. The cosmic eroticism involved expresses in its own fashion the duality of death and life within a mixed infinite. . . . They [the generating divinities] remind us in a perfect manner, suggestive of the cosmic union which integrates the collective individual in a globality that surpasses him."[14] He also gives an undiluted definition of the surreal: "a form of the real that is particularly concrete, which is involved to the highest point with everyday existence."[15]

In applying his philosophy of immanence to poetics, Breton's greatest contribution is probably his revolutionary modification of the art of representation—a field of highest interest to the end-of-the-century critics.[16] That much maligned poem, "L'Union libre," myopically taken to refer "poetically to his wife's private parts" (note that it was written at a time when Breton had no wife!), implements the most important of Breton's aesthetic theories: that of poetic representation, whereby he transformed a stereotype blason into a courtship between human form and function and the ecology. Scholars currently searching for distinctions between mimetic versus transformational representation and so-called re-presentation are rethinking André Breton, yet most of them are admittedly unaware of Breton's work in this area. Any thinking on this subject could profitably use as preliminary texts "L'Union libre" and the essay "Signe ascendant."

Among those who have written on Breton there have been two strong lines of approach: the ecstatic and the belligerent. On the one hand there occurs such an overwhelming empathy that the commentary assumes the very language of the commentated text and assimilates Breton's ideology. Such commentary often becomes heavy with Breton's intentionalities. The other tone is that of those who embrace Dada and Surrealism as part of the larger avant-garde movements of the time but are uncomfortable with Breton. They are apt to accuse him of hypocrisy, of super-human posturing. They attack his *point sublime* but sound as if they discovered the expression in secondary sources. Were they to go to *L'Amour fou* they would realize that in that supremely moving letter of Breton to his little daughter *point sublime* had to do with Breton's humble perception of the unattainable mountain peak: "There was never any question of my settling there. Besides, in that respect, it would have ceased to be sublime and I would have ceased to be a man."[17]

What has not yet been clearly recognized is the role André Breton played in the global literary adjustment to the modern world. He started as an avant-garde writer but consolidated his position in a comprehensive accommodation to the concept of the relativity of reality over and above the ancient dichotomy between the real and the unreal. He was perhaps the only one in that first wave of the avant-garde of the twentieth century to proceed to the formation of a guard, knowing that this avant-garde is always preliminary.

Instead of rejecting beauty, as did many avant-garde writers and painters, Breton tried to redefine it in terms of "convulsive" beauty. Instead of rejecting mimesis, he established a non-anthropocentric relationship with the ecology, absorbing it into an elaborate, intricate system of analogies with the human sensorial system and in a deeper understanding of what nature has come to mean; and he also endeavored to explain the unpredictable manifestations of chance. In the questionnaire he was asked to fill out—that unique document I mentioned above—he stressed under the caption "Major areas of vocational interests, etc." his lifelong "struggle which aims to recast human understanding, starting with the proposition to modify sensibility." He ends the statement with an upbeat sense of success. Contrary to his initial instinct to abandon the notion of "literary" completely, he ultimately came to terms with a redefinition which he believed necessary to the term "literature" to make it acceptable in this age. It could survive as the expression of a close linkage with sociology to reveal a "passionate" knowledge of human behavior. This interest included a strong commitment to the salutary potential of women, which anti-Bretonian feminists might want to read before they accuse Breton of being anti-feminist. "This eternal power of woman, the only one before which I have ever bowed," he wrote in *L'Amour fou,* and he elaborated on this statement in *Arcane 17* after having written some of the most passionate love poems of this century. These two prose texts should be required reading in every bibliography of women's studies. José Pierre's essay in this volume, "Such Is Beauty," focuses on this motivating interface of Breton's life and work.

Another adaptation of literature to modern concerns was Breton's interest in madness, but it was more oriented toward social attitudes than toward purely psychological insights or psychotherapy. The plight of the "deranged" was applicable to the broader and more universally inclusive metaphor of the prison house in which humans so often feel confined. His abandonment of Nadja was perceived by him not as the behavior of the moral cad – as some of his commentators have viewed it – but as the deplorable consequence of his inability to cope with the free spirit embodied by Nadja and with which, despite all his efforts, he could not totally identify because of the strictures inculcated in him by society as well as by his unbending rationality. If society as a whole did not know how to handle the problem of the "deranged" except by incarceration, the situation was to him a valid subject for literature rather than a merely clinical problem; in this respect again, Latin American writers such as Julio Cortazar, Rosamel del Valle, and Enrique Gómez-Correa have followed in Breton's direction.

In his little-known *Sociología de la locura* (The Sociology of Madness) the Chilean Enrique Gómez-Correa – poet, literary scholar, lawyer, psychologist – considers the multiple facets of the state of mind that extend beyond the rational boundaries; he weighs the clinical symptoms, the poetic manifestations, and the legal repercussions of society's mishandling of the deranged. He concludes that "poetic knowledge, both literary and philosophical, gives us an idea that is more direct about the same phenomenon of insanity, more substantial, more profound than all those descriptions of psychiatry and formal psychology."[18] He salutes the Surrealists and particularly André Breton for having stirred what he considers the most fundamental problems of the human condition: "The Surrealists in the temporal affirmations have done nothing short of placing on a bloody table the capital problems of man."[19] His credibility lies in the fact that he comes to this conclusion after perusing an extraordinary range of references in literature, philosophy, psychology, and a number of other disciplines, as well as the penal codes of several countries.

The discourse of the dream state and of the in-between area of the conscious and the unconscious was probably best exemplified in the poetry of Robert Desnos, and in Buñuel's many translations of the dream to the screen. James Joyce got much better results with the stream of consciousness in the area of narrative prose than did the Surrealists. Breton, however, succeeded in conveying in *Nadja* the state of mad vision in some of the dialogue he reports with his uncanny companion, who sees a "blue wind"; blue, according to Dr. Pierre Janet and confirmed by Gómez-Correa's observations, is the predominant color in paintings by the deranged. But it is the virtually neglected Chilean poet Rosamel del Valle who in *Eva y la fuga* gives a prose narrative collage of the irrational with the rational, exceeding the dimensions of the aberrations conveyed in *Nadja*. In Gómez-Correa's opinion, the collaboration of Breton and Éluard in *L'Immaculée Conception* was the best simulation of the perception of the irrational in literature. In Jacqueline Chénieux-Gendron's article, "Toward a New Definition of Automatism: *L'Immaculée Conception*," which appears in this volume, we have the latest illumination on this work and its particular uses of automatic resources. In general, however, studies on the irrational in surrealist literature concentrate on the theoretical revelations of the texts rather than on the degree of irrational expression achieved by the work. Thus, Breton's comments *about* the irrational rather than his attempts to convey it are quoted. In my own scrutinies of Breton texts I have found him most successful in demonstrating the passage, the shuttle from the rational to the irrational, the basic continuum rather than the contrasting character of two separate states, and a resulting vision of confluence which I believe to be scientifically a truer one than the older insistence on a dichotomy.

Breton was at his best when he dealt with the concordance of chance with human desire, of which he felt the need, like many other moderns, in confronting a gratuitous universe. In the entire course of his writing he forced verbal encounters as springboards to his thoughts. Even in terms of the conception of his child he vied with chance: "Ma toute petite enfant . . . tout hasard a été rigoureusement exclu de votre venue."[20] For him there was no drifting along with chance but an active manipulation of it. In the very same epoch in which Sartre presented Roquentin in a quandary, paralyzed by the recognition of a world of inconsequence, Breton was retaliating against the same situation. His affirmative attitude in the face of the *"Néant"* in the Heideggerian thirties made him one of the few who reacted positively rather than despairingly to a non-anthropocentric universe.

Finally, let us remember that Breton's contribution in the field of the visual arts has perhaps been the most universally acknowledged and pervasive aspect of his influence. Not only was he quick to appreciate the new directions of his immediate elders, but he catalyzed his contemporaries and discovered talents which a large public was later to acclaim in confirmation of his judgment. He also found in the process a new form of aesthetic criticism: how to *read* painting, distancing himself and some of his group from standard art criticism. I think that is what the late J. H. Matthews's essay here on Arshile Gorky makes evident. What Breton taught his contemporaries, both the poets and the painters, was not simply the juxtaposition of distant realities but the exploration and appropriation of objects. An interdisciplinary scholar such as Inez Hedges has shown in her book *Languages of Revolt*[21] what impact Breton may have had on contemporary artists and filmmakers who continue to apply his principles beyond the original surrealist coterie. Renée Riese Hubert in her *Surrealism and the Book,*[22] which deals with the concerted, intertwined work of graphic/verbal associations epitomized in Surrealism, gives the long history that culminates in the notion of reading painting as the convergence of interpretive methods of reading the open text of the visual and the verbal together.

Completing the inventory of Breton's poetic structures that have been or should be subjected to scholarly analysis and reader response is the poem-object, which at first was perceived as an effort on the part of non-artists to use visuals to express thought in figurative form. In the latest collection of essays that has reached me before this modest "bilan" goes to press, *L'Objet au défi,*[23] compiled by Jacqueline Chénieux-Gendron and containing responses to the metaphoric and what I call "interartifactuality" of Surrealism, there is an article by José Pierre on Breton's concept and achievement in respect to the poem-object. As he takes account of theory and practice, he surmises that beyond the act of casting bridges between the interior and exterior worlds, Breton's poem-object attempts to fuse time separations, turning art into event, giving a phenomenological character to its revelatory function. In this important volume, linguists and philosophers have seriously appraised the implications of that caricature of reality so often associated with surrealist art that reaches beyond ironic laughter, aroused by paradox, to resonate with the tragic that lies beyond despair. In each of these essays Breton remains the constant interface. In our current volume, Martine Antle goes so far as to suggest in "Breton, Portrait and Anti-Portrait" that Breton himself became a poem-object for his artist-contemporaries.

What does the immediate future seem to promise in the way of Breton scholarship? The most welcome collaborative scholarship beyond the American Dada/Surrealism Association's work is that of C.A.S. (Champs des Activités Surréalistes) under the auspices of the Centre National des Recherches Scientifiques in conjunction with the University of Paris. It has produced two regular journals, *Signes* and *Pleine Marge,* collected the surrealist tracts, reproduced the important and out-of-print journals of the Surrealists, organized colloquia, published academic studies, and kept an up-to-date bibliography of works printed and in progress. Among collaborators on this team are Jacqueline Chénieux-Gendron, M. C. Dumas, José Pierre, José Vovelle, and of course the most assiduous of Breton scholars, Marguerite Bonnet. Another surrealist journal is *Mélusine*, under the direction of Henri Béhar, professor and former president of Paris III. His essay here, "The Passionate Attraction," casts light on the mysterious actress who fascinated Breton, an attraction which was symptomatic of a greater interest in the theatre than is generally attributed to him.

It is clear that scholarly activity on Breton is increasing although among academics in the U.S.A. he does not enjoy the popularity of Georges Bataille or Raymond Roussel. One might also note that a comprehensive avant-garde conference at Hofstra University in November 1986 demonstrated that among younger scholars interest in Duchamp and Dada far surpassed interest in Breton.

But among poets and artists, empathy with Breton runs much higher than among scholars. Linguists, psychocritics and reception theoreticians will no doubt enlarge our knowledge and enjoyment of Breton's work or assess Breton's contribution to the modern mentality and to the direction of intellectual change when they begin to treat his poetry—as they have Mallarmé's—with the methodology suitable for a polysemantic work, prohibitive of unilateral deciphering. Michael Riffaterre's explication of an excerpt from *Poisson soluble* illustrates here how far afield such decoding virtuosity can lead. Let us keep in mind in reading him that what he attributes to the reader's detective capacity is his own particular and personal interpretation, or as Dali would say, "delirium of interpretation," through "intertexts" which are of his choosing, spring out of his mind, and which do not have to limit the much broader range of the poetic field which Breton opens up to his readers. The power of the poetry of Breton to survive is precisely due to its dense character, which allows reception on multiple levels and is sustainable in different historical eras. Standard analytic methodologies are unlikely to reduce to rational, linear structures Breton's prisms and mosaics. The circularity of his work leaves him forever impermeable if he does not at the same time provoke passion in the respondent.

This collection of essays is dedicated to the memory of J. H. Matthews, whose seminal books and exemplary commitment to the field of Surrealism will continue to inspire us.

I would like to thank Rudolf Kuenzli for his collaboration in conceiving and editing this collection, Esther Allen for her excellent translations, Gail Zlatnik for her generous and superb editorial assistance, and Judith Pendleton for her great artistic sense and care.

Notes

1. See Robert Champigny, "Une Définition du surréalisme," in *Pour une esthétique de l'essai* (Paris: Lettres Modernes, Minard, 1967).

2. "La violence de certaines expressions polémiques dans le texte de 1930 m'oblige aujourd'hui à des réserves, en fonction du devenir des uns et des autres (je ne pense pas seulement à Artaud, à Desnos)," in a letter of September 15, 1945, which is part of the dossier of Léon Pierre-Quint, which his sister, Françoise Selz, deposited at the Bibliothèque Nationale.

3. Michael Riffaterre in *La Production du texte* (Paris: Seuil, 1979).

4. Renée Riese Hubert, "*Nadja* depuis la mort de Breton," *Oeuvres et critiques, 2, 1: Prose romanesque du 20ᵉ siècle* (Spring 1977), 93–102.

5. Breton not only pressed Léon Pierre-Quint to bring this work back into print but in *Entretiens* he admits that he has retained a special weakness for *Les Vases communicants* (p. 169).

6. Michel Beaujour, "André Breton et la transparence," in *Arcane 17* (Paris: Pauvert, 1965).

7. See P. Mourier-Casile, *André Breton explorateur de la Mère-Moire: trois lectures d' "Arcane 17"* (Paris: Presses universitaires de France, 1986).

8. This questionnaire was used for the entry on Breton in the *Contemporary Authors* series of Gale Research Company.

9. See J. D. Hubert, "André Breton et le paradis perdu," *French Review* (December 1963), 200–205.

10. See Anna Balakian, "Continuity and Discontinuity in the Poetics of Ambiguity," in *Writings in a Modern Temper*, ed. Mary Ann Caws (Stanford: Stanford University Press, 1984).

11. See Riffaterre, "Intertextualité surréaliste," *Mélusine* 1 (1979), 27–37.

12. "*Fata Morgana* m'a enchanté; le poème est d'une rare douceur et peut-être celui par lequel vous vous exprimez le plus complètement. Les thèmes se succèdent avec une richesse et une beauté impressionnantes." Dated October 2, 1941, in the Selz Collection.

13. Michel Maffesoli, *L'Ombre de Dionysos* (Paris: Méridiens/Anthropos, 1982), 75.

14. Ibid., 80.

15. Maffesoli, *La Conquête du présent* (Paris: Presses universitaires de France, 1979), 80.

16. See Stamos Metzidakis, *Repetition and Semiotics* (Birmingham, Alabama: Summa Publications, 1986).

17. André Breton, *L'Amour fou* (Paris: Gallimard, 1937), 134.

18. Enrique Gómez-Correa, *Sociología de la locura* (Santiago, Chile: Aire Libre, 1942), 131.

19. Ibid., 125.

20. Breton, *L'Amour fou*, 130.

21. See Inez Hedges, *Languages of Revolt* (Durham: Duke University Press, 1983).

22. See Renée Riese Hubert, *Surrealism and the Book* (Berkeley: University of California Press, 1987).

23. See *L'Objet au défi,* ed. Jacqueline Chénieux-Gendron and Marie-Claire Dumas (Paris: Presses universitaires de France, 1987).

The Passionate Attraction: André Breton and the Theatre

Henri Béhar

In the name of the truth of beings, André Breton rejects the theatre's two masks, the one the playwright must put on to create a character as well as the one the actor wears to play a role. No fiction is tolerable to Breton, be it dramatic or narrative.

Nevertheless, he showed no reluctance to attend the theatre, particularly the so aptly named Theatre of the Two Masks, which he writes about in *Nadja*. Nor was he later reluctant to defend certain playwrights, such as Julien Gracq, Georges Schéhadé, Eugène Ionesco, and Henri Pichette, all of whom seemed to him to incarnate the individual truth he sought. He also defended society's outcast, Antonin Artaud. Moreover, he himself, in collaboration with the companions of his youth, was the perpetrator of four plays which he never repudiated, even if he never made any particular effort to have them produced. Before his death, he requested that two of his plays, *Vous m'oublierez* and *S'il vous plaît* (the fourth act of which had never been published), be added to the 1967 reedition of the founding text of Surrealism, *Les Champs magnétiques*. It is thus evident that a certain ambiguity, made of attraction and repulsion, characterizes Breton's relationship to the theatre. Let us try to elucidate that ambiguity.

I don't know why – I have no new findings to prove it – but Breton's first contacts with Tzara have always appeared to me to have to do with a project which was theatrical, in all senses of the word. They were attempting, it seems to me, to cause a great disruption, and hence to use the theatre, which was at the time, and for several years afterwards, the best way of activating the public, far better than literature or silent film.

Breton wrote to his new friend in Zurich, "To kill art appears to me to be of the utmost urgency, but we cannot operate in the open" (4 April 1919). The common goal is evident, but the strategy has not yet been adopted. Should they act openly, as the Dadaists had done in Switzerland since 1916 or rather, as Breton suggests, should they proceed by means of a secret society of writers whose subversive impact would be no less radical? Soon after, Breton confided to Tzara: "I'm writing very little right now, and am ripening a project which should upset several worlds. Don't think that this is childish or delirious. But the preparation of a *coup d'état* can take several years" (20 April 1919).

According to Marguerite Bonnet, it was at the end of that same April and until the middle of June that the adventure, with Philippe Soupault, of writing what would become *Les Champs magnétiques* took place. I continue to insist that *Les Champs magnétiques* has as much to do with the theatre as with poetry, in the way it establishes a new form of dialogue between two minds, in the way it merges their suddenly crystallizing thoughts. The chapter titled "Barriers" displays the surrealist desire to "reestablish the dialogue in its absolute truth, by releasing the two interlocutors from the obligations of common politeness," as Breton put it in the *Manifesto*. At the time, nothing was certain, and it was not known if the pages of automatic writing would even be worth printing. On the other hand, the new technique is immediately extended into the form of a play, *S'il vous plaît,* a drama in four acts written by the same collaborators; Breton announced its completion on 26 December 1919, expressing the desire to "have it performed next spring" (14 January 1920).

I firmly believe that there is no solution to the problem of continuity from *Les Champs magnétiques* to *S'il vous plaît* and *Vous m'oublierez,* though all three texts are integrated into the same strategy for a *coup d'état* which was fomenting in Paris, near Val-de-Grace, in 1919.

What was the prospective revolution aimed at? At toppling art from its pedestal? That was the least of it. The paradox, experienced by Dada, was that to reach this end you had to employ artistic means. Unless you made of automatism an end and not a means, the theatre was, in some way, the revelation or the catalyst of this direct grasp of thought. That is how the lyrical, poetic, unexpected utterance insinuates itself into the dramatic form and contaminates it, as the exquisite cadaver contaminates rational argumentation. The dramaturgy is one of discontinuity, the perturbation of logic, the antagonism between word and gesture – all underhanded devices designed to explode the theatre, to make it dissolve.

But Breton's and Soupault's intentions were far more serious than the published text would lead us to believe. They were as serious as life itself. The authors were inclined to gamble their lives in an onstage game of Russian roulette, thus annulling the distance between the theatre and its double. In the absence of an immediate and dazzling victory over the public, the ever-fascinating death wish presented itself.

Fortunately, the emotional community of the Dadaists, and a love affair, turned Breton against this lethal scheme, and against any desperate violence.

That this temptation, once overcome, alienated Breton from the theatre is easily understood. But it was not enough to make him shun absolutely

14

any theatrical presentation. I tried to account for Breton's strange interest in a *grand guignol* play, *Les Détraquées,* which he saw several times at the Theatre of the Two Masks, and which he wrote about at length in *Nadja.*[1] Neither his willed perversity, nor the desire to defend a work which had been disparaged, seemed to me to justify the detailed account of this play which he gives. Only the atmosphere of the theatre, the staging, the acting, the intimate emotion of the spectator could have given rise to such admiration. Thinking of the definitive words pronounced by Breton to describe Blanche Derval, "the most admirable and without a doubt the *only* actress of our time," I wanted to know more about this actress whose name I had never seen elsewhere, a name which echoed that of the author of *Les Filles du feu* too closely not to be fictional. Without much hope, I was pulling on the Ariadne thread of my investigation when a friend of mine, a daughter of a member of the Society of the Comédie Française, questioned her mother on my behalf and informed me that Blanche Derval was probably living in a retirement home, and gave me the address of someone who could put me in touch with her. I wrote immediately and received no response. I was going to resume my investigations in another direction when I received, anonymously, a page printed on both sides and folded in quarters, bearing this title: NADJA BLANCHE. On it were four letters from André Breton to Blanche Derval, two photographs of the latter taken at the time of *Les Détraquées,* and the facsimiles of dedications from Breton to Blanche Derval written on the *Manifeste du Surréalisme* and on *Nadja.* An eight-line note, signed "G.L.," gave the reason for this somewhat clandestine publication: to definitively put an end to any identification between Blanche and Nadja.

I never had the chance to thank (which I do here) the overly discreet sender of this missive that came to satisfy my professional curiosity, and I did not try to identify him or her.

Breton had not contented himself with procuring, from the Studio Henri Manuel, the onstage photograph and the portrait of Blanche which appear in *Nadja;* he had tried several times to contact the actress.

The first time, on 29 January 1922, while the preparations were under way for the International Congress for the Determination of the Directives and the Defense of the Modern Spirit, called the Congress of Paris, he solicited her collaboration: "It is to you and you alone that we made this request, because we know of no one other than you who incarnates the modern spirit in the theatre today. . . ." Breton received no response to this letter. Nonetheless, the terms used in *Nadja,* which are consonant with these, can be explained by the fact that the actress was the only person, in the eyes of her admirer, to incarnate modernity in the theatre. The letter contains no mention of her role, nor of the authors of the play that Breton would publish in the first issue of *Le Surréalisme même* in 1956.

The three other letters date from the time when the author was endeavoring to assemble the photographic documentation which would "eliminate all description" from his narrative.

It appears that Breton took the liberty of dropping in on the actress at her home, with no advance notice. He excuses and explains himself in a letter sent immediately afterwards: "I am about to publish, as I briefly told you, a work which is, properly speaking, neither an essay nor a novel, in the course of which I evoke, among other significant and decisive episodes of my life, two or three evenings which I once spent at the Two Masks, and I speak of you, and you alone, in this connection" (14 September 1927).

Offering to read her the passage which concerns her and to comment in person on the circumstances, he concludes with several admiring phrases whose tone clearly goes beyond the obligations of common politeness.

Several days later, another letter, which the actress received at the Municipal Theatre of La-Roche-sur-Yon where she was on tour, thanks her for her authorization to use the photographs he wishes to procure: "Yours first, Madame, because I have admired you more than any artist in the world, which I state with unmistakable clarity in my book, and then one of a scene from the play as well, because my memories of it will never fade" (26 September 1927).

The last letter, received under the same circumstances at the Municipal Theatre of Niort, indicates that Breton has procured the photographs from the Studio Henri Manuel, and requests additional information on the actress's career. Breton comments: "These photographs of *Les Détraquées* are far from giving me the extraordinary impression which certain episodes in the play left on me, and above all certain expressions which I saw you adopt during it. Such as they are, though, they are still infinitely moving, and I thank you for having given me the means of confronting my faithful and passionate memory of several evenings at the Two Masks with this all too fixed and objective a test" (2 October 1927).

In *Nadja*, Breton chose to reproduce the most neutral portrait of Blanche, the one which best conforms to the conventions of the time, preferring it over the photos lent to him, which incorporate a play of mirrors and are reproduced in the leaflet I have described above. More than five years after seeing the play, the impression is still just as vivid, and the writer seems to relive his emotions as he transcribes only what floats to the surface.

Without challenging the rules of etiquette, and with the greatest respect for the actress's privacy, Breton attempted to prolong this epistolary encounter. But, at the same time, politeness alone does not seem to justify the reserve he evinced after the theatrical spectacle which so moved him.

Here is the sequence of events: Breton goes to see *Les Détraquées* two or three times. There, he undergoes an unparalleled emotional shock, attempts to associate the actress who is the cause of this shock with his project of questioning the modern spirit and, for lack of a response, makes no further attempt at that time. Then the experience of writing *Nadja* makes him relive the initial experience of the play. So he makes contact for the second time with the woman who inspired his greatest theatrical passion, and, doubtless for lack of the least movement of understanding from his correspondent, restricts himself to what can pass for a great deference.

The book, "swinging like a door," opens out onto life. Breton had not, indeed, heard Blanche Derval's name mentioned again when he wrote *Nadja*, but he contacted her personally when he was readying the book for printing.

If he does not modify the phrase "of whom, perhaps to my great shame, I have never heard anything again," to account for the exchange which I have just related, it is because the past has not modified the present course of life. In 1962, he tries to explain this phrase and his attitude by the following addition: "What did I mean? That I should have approached her, tried at any price to unveil the real *woman* that she was. To do that, I would have had to overcome certain prejudices against actresses which the memory of Vigny and Nerval bore out. I reproach myself in that instance for not having been equal to the 'passionate attraction.'"

In short, the mask of the role was never removed. Breton chides himself for not having removed it, overdetermined as he was by a romantic vision of the diabolical actress, sucking the poet's life away. Marie Dorval prevented him from knowing the true Blanche Derval.

But he was not prevented from dreaming of her, as the dedication inscribed on 27 September 1927 on a copy of the *Manifeste du Surréalisme* testifies. As strange as it may appear to associate a manifesto with the dream of a woman, Breton's behavior can be understood from the famous phrase "It is living and ceasing to live which are the imaginary solutions." The stage was for this ideal spectator, on one certain occasion, the place of existence. Then the curtain fell, forever.

Fourier used the expression "passionate attraction" – or "impassioned" – to designate the vocations which direct every person toward a particular employment. By a slight shift in meaning, Breton uses it in a more general way to name the feeling that he should have developed for the actress.

For my part, I very willingly see it as the ambivalent sign of his attitude toward the theatre. On the one hand, he expects from it a revelation, or at least a great find. This is his attitude towards the Modern Theatre, of which he speaks in *Nadja*, which he frequented at one point because it was the scene of the theatrical counter-ritual; because in it the spectator could be active and no longer passive; because the actors played against their roles, trying to establish contact with the audience; because the decor of the theatre made him think of Rimbaud's taste for the modern. The encounter with the actress took place in a similar establishment, of a

17

slightly better kind, and we have seen the force with which that encounter marked a spectator who was open to it and given to reverie. With *Les Détraquées*, Breton's attention focuses on the stage. The play seems to him to be exclusively of the dramatic genre, as much in its content as in the performances of the actors. And he has eyes only for the actress, whose expressions are for him the source of great mystery.

But, on the other hand, there is the irrevocable condemnation found in *Introduction au discours sur le peu de réalité* of the two masks of which I spoke above. The theatrical game is impossible from both sides. The passionate attraction can lead, at best, only to frustration, at worst, to a passionate repulsion. It seems that the marvelous has been overridden by reason and the demands of morality – an astonishing thing in a man whose independence of mind is well established.

The prejudice Breton felt towards the actress must be understood in a larger context, as the legacy of Rousseau's notion that the theatre is a place of isolation and affectation: "We believe we have assembled in the theatre, yet it is there that we isolate ourselves; it is there that we go to forget our friends, our neighbors, our families, and to immerse ourselves in fables, to weep for the misfortunes of dead men, or laugh at the expense of the living" (Rousseau: *Lettre à d'Alembert*).

Breton's considerations on the economic and social aspects of the theatre which, according to him, lead to the worst compromises, appear to me to be quite secondary in light of the demand for truth, which would have the art of the theatre return to the popular festival: "Give the spectators the stage; make them actors themselves" (Rousseau, *Lettre à d'Alembert*).

Certainly the theatre can and must become an instrument of social cohesion, but its magical origins endow it with many other functions which Surrealism could have explored. The experiments of the Theatre Alfred-Jarry provide sufficient evidence of this. It is a pity that Breton's prejudices against it prevented him from following or even directing the course of Antonin Artaud's enterprise towards the theatre of cruelty. Artaud's initiatives, though not without relation to the fundamental ambitions of the surrealist movement, were developed at a distance from it. There again, the passionate attraction should have been in the theatre's favor.

Translated by Esther Allen

Note

1. In my *Le Théâtre dada et surréaliste* (Paris: Gallimard, 1979).

"Such Is Beauty":
The "Convulsive" in Breton's
Ethics and Aesthetics

José Pierre

In his "Souvenirs of Mexico," published in May 1939 in the last issue of *Minotaure*,[1] André Breton describes at length the seductive effect that the discovery in the city of Guadalajara of an edifice as splendid as it was dilapidated had on him. He calls it both the "palace of fatality" and the "Slum Palace" (Palais-Masure), and its seduction draws him back for a second look:

> Before leaving the city, I wanted to see the Slum Palace again, for fear of forgetting some aspect of it, of losing the key which would open it up for me from far away. An emotion such as I have never felt before, made all the stronger and intensified from instant to instant by the certitude that I would never feel it again, awaited me on the other side of the drawing room door. At that hour of the morning the blinds were lowered over thick red curtains, and the massive wooden space of the room was dark and immensely empty, although it still contained a piano. A lovely creature, sixteen or seventeen years old and ideally disheveled, who had come to open the door for me, stood there alone. After she put down her broom, she smiled a smile from the dawn of the world in which there was not a trace of confusion. She moved with a supreme ease: her gestures, which were as troubling as they were harmonious, revealed her to be naked under her ragged white evening gown. The fascination she held for me at that moment was such that I neglected to find out anything about her identity: who could she be? The daughter or the sister of one of the beings who had frequented these regions during the time of their splendor? Or was she of the invading race? It did not matter: as long as she was there I could not have cared less about her origin, it was enough for me to give thanks for her existence. *Such is beauty.*[2]

This radiant apparition not only offers us a striking image of *desire*, but also reminds us of how attached Breton had become to the notion of relating the process of amorous emotion to that of artistic emotion, to the point of making this relationship one of the fundamentals of his theoretical and critical thought. In 1928, in the last pages of *Nadja*, he exclaimed: "Beauty will be CONVULSIVE or will not be," an affirmation which is repeated and amplified in 1937, in an obscure and peremptory form, in *L'Amour fou:* "Convulsive beauty will be erotic-veiled, explosive-permanent, magic-circumstantial or will not be."[3] Certainly, the "beauty" he speaks of here is that which chiefly characterizes the artistic and poetic works which won from Breton an adherence as intense as it was immediate. But it is clear that he is also speaking of the feeling excited by a woman who is loved or simply desired; the young Mexican of the Slum Palace can serve as the proof of this. Moreover, in *L'Amour fou* Breton has underlined the similarity of the two situations in the clearest possible way when he writes:

I admit without the least confusion that I am profoundly unmoved in the presence of natural sights and works of art which do not straightaway give me the sensation of a slight breeze like the passing of an egret at my temples capable of causing a real shiver. I have never been able to prevent myself from establishing a relationship between this sensation and that of erotic pleasure, and the only difference I see between them is one of degree.[4]

This "difference of degree" poses, of course, the problem of *sublimation,* which Breton never tried to evade, but which Freud, as we know, never addressed in anything more than the most summary fashion.

It might seem surprising that Breton would try to extend his most intimate predispositions to the whole surrealist *egregore,* as if the observations resulting from his own experience could serve as the springboard of a collective verification. But he wrote in *L'Amour fou:* "Each time a man loves, he inevitably engages the sensibility of all men along with his own. In order not to be unworthy of them, he owes it to himself to engage it fully."[5]

When he stated in 1928 that beauty should be "convulsive," Breton clearly meant that all of Surrealism should make itself, or recognize itself as, "convulsive." Hardly had this veritable act of faith been formulated than the most "convulsive" of all the surrealist painters, Salvador Dali, made his entrance into the group. In 1947, in an attempt to define the most telling characteristic of the implications of Surrealism for the plastic arts, Breton would write: "Whether or not the positions that we took, on painting, for example, are disputed, I think that Surrealism did not fail to carry out the first item on its agenda, which is to endow the plastic arts with the capacity of ceaselessly recreating themselves in order to translate the continual fluctuations of human desire."[6] Obviously, "human desire" goes far beyond "amorous desire," but amorous desire remains the essential reference and the interior model of human desire. This becomes even clearer when Breton sums up the thesis of *L'Amour fou,* declaring:

I have worked for nothing so much as the demonstration of what precautions and what ruses desire, in search of its object, employs as it angles through the waters of preconsciousness, and, once the object is found, of what means – stupefying, until we learn better – it disposes for making that object known to consciousness.[7]

"Desire, the world's one force, desire, the one rigor with which man must acquaint himself,"[8] should, nonetheless, not conceal from us all that opposes it, and equally opposes the facility with which Surrealism in its entirety is designated as the place where desire is fulfilled and its writing (or painting) is designated the writing (or painting) of desire. This designation is not false, but it is at once hasty and insufficient. Jules Monnerot demonstrated this when, discussing Maurice Nadeau's *History of Surrealism,* he wrote:

"The true revolution is the victory of desire," affirms M. Nadeau in a nutshell. But what if desire is opposed to itself? He forgets that Surrealism wished to be "a cry of the spirit which turns back towards itself . . . with the intention of desperately smashing its shackles." The antinomies which exist in Surrealism's deepest intention cannot be reconciled through the language of rational justification: they are lived through the cyclical alternation of hope and despair, night and day, aspiration and expiration.[9]

In the same way, it would not have been enough for the Surrealists simply to question their sexuality[10] or to ask the question: What sort of hope do you place (do we place) in love?[11] And Breton, in his preface to the 1933 reedition of Achim von Arnim's *Contes bizarres,* after having examined what he takes for a "disaster"—the relationship between the German writer and his wife Bettina—concludes:

The sexual world, in our time, despite the explorations which the modern era has sent into it (of which those of Sade and Freud are the most memorable), has not to my knowledge ceased to oppose to our will to penetrate the universe its own unshatterable kernel of *night.*[12]

This "unshatterable kernel of *night,*" however disheartening the acknowledgment of its existence might be, serves to make the glimpses of daylight granted by a shared love all the more dazzling. Desire would lose all of its interest if it succeeded in ridding itself of its nocturnal aspect. Or if it were to comply with the wishes of those who advocate an "unshackled orgasm" of pure animality. As for Georges Bataille's *black* eroticism, the least that can be said of it is that it develops not only the "night" of desire but also its "unshatterable" aspect to the utmost possible degree (see, for example, *Madame Edwarda*). Breton, without concealing the somber aspect of love (Baudelaire had already said that the greatest pleasure of love consisted in the certitude of doing evil), takes a position which is the contrary of Bataille's, and though he doesn't try to bring it into full daylight (which would be a demented enterprise), he does attempt to shed at least some light on it. Instead of finding his path, like Bataille, only in Sade's direction (or even in that of the tradition of mysticism which adapts itself, like the delirium of Sade's heroes, to the annihilation of the human being with the goal of acceding to *ecstasy*), Breton looked as well, and contradictorily (someone else might say dialectically), towards the tradition of courtly love and German romanticism (where, at the extreme opposite of sadism, the divinization of the beloved woman is accomplished at the price of a more or less pronounced renunciation of carnal enjoyment). In this sense, the indispensable auxiliary to Breton is Freud, interrogated with an unfailing vigilance.

In 1930, in the *Second Surrealist Manifesto,* Breton had designated a "sublime point" at which all the contradictions which analytic reasoning held as irreconcilable would be annulled, as the supreme objective of Surrealism; in the same way, Breton sketched an amorous itinerary (in short, a new "Carte de tendre") where courtly love and Sade, Novalis and Freud would "cease to be perceived as contradictory." The love he advocates would in no case renounce the pleasures of the flesh:

Love, the only love which is, carnal love, I adore and have never ceased adoring your venomous shadow, your fatal shadow. A day will come when man will be able to recognize you as his sole master and honor you even for the mysterious perversions with which you surround him.[13]

But the celebration of this "poisonous shadow" of love is necessarily accompanied by a denunciation of "the vile Christian notion of sin. There has never been a forbidden fruit. Temptation alone is divine."[14] To which statement, however, Breton adds, so that there will be no confusion between his own attitude and that of the libertine: "To experience the need to vary the object of this temptation, to replace it by others, is to demonstrate a readiness to be unworthy, and doubtless already an unworthiness of *innocence.* Innocence in the sense of absolute non-culpability."[15]

If the theme of elective love emerges with force at this moment, as well as the sacred aura which surrounds it, the defiant attitude will become more nuanced with time, as is evident in this important statement made in 1964, at a time when a "sexual revolution" was already widely discussed:

Under the sovereign pressure of Freud's ideas, we are now more and more willing to agree that sexuality leads the world. From which it appears to result that everyone should be precipitately lifted above the taboos and interdictions which, with their postponement of gratification from one time and place to others, weigh no less heavily on primitive peoples than on us. The repercussions of the discoveries of psychoanalysis have been such that it was inevitable that the most absolute incompetence, or even indignity, was attached to this problem. In the uncharted darkness which is always virtually total in this area, these are the voices which give us their suggestions, as ridiculous as they are perilous, in the matter of sexual education. It seems nonetheless that the youth of a certain country, in this respect more liberated than any other, has proven as well to be more bewildered. Systematic sexual education is worthwhile only insofar as it leaves intact the forces of "sublimation" and finds a means of surmounting the attraction of the "forbidden fruit." It could only be a form of initiation – with all of the notions of the sacred that the word supposes (though of course without religion) – and with its implication that the ideal constitution of each couple incorporates an element of quest. *Love can be retained only at this price.*[16]

Thirty years later, we rediscover here ("in the uncharted darkness which is always virtually total in this area") the echo of the "unshatterable kernel of *night*" of 1933. However, in respect now to the text of *L'Amour fou,* a perceptible difference exists as regards the "forbidden fruit" and more generally all "taboos and interdictions." First of all (and this is what so many neophytes, who take literally certain surrealist passwords which only made sense in respect to what they were opposing at a given moment, refuse to understand), Breton did not cease to take into account the modification of mentalities, and it is quite certain that the menaces which threatened love in 1964 were no longer the same as those it had confronted in 1933 or 1937: the time of strictness had been succeeded by a time of laxness in which we are more or less still living. Moreover, Breton was extremely attentive to the latest developments of Bataille's reflections on eroticism, to the point of referring directly to them in the introductory text of the 1959 International Exposition of Surrealism, which had chosen eroticism as its structuring theme. Pointedly citing the following sentence by Bataille, "The interior experience of eroticism demands of the person who undergoes it a sensitivity to the anguish on which the interdiction is grounded which is as great as the sensitivity to the desire which attempts to break down the interdiction," he commented on it in these terms:

This interdiction, which is immemorial and continues to impose itself on us, at every latitude, from the so-called "savages" to the so-called "civilizations," is, in effect, the true focal point of eroticism. We consider that its shape will become clearer as the immense undergrowth of prejudices which conceals it is removed. At the same time, it would be foolish to wish to bring it out into full daylight. Whoever believes he can brave prejudice and interdiction at once without turning a hair will find himself no longer fit to deal with eroticism because he will have misunderstood the fundamental need in his own consciousness for *transgression.*[17]

Of course Breton did not fail to continue by reestablishing once again his *distance* from Bataille:

In this respect, all is not necessarily as black as Bataille would have it, which does not prevent his analysis from being among the most valuable, *at the extreme.* The triggering device of eroticism within the human soul does not perhaps require this superabundance of contradictory energies where only the pleasure-suffering pair can succeed in sublimating itself in complete fusion. Here we are forced to take into account individual complexions and diverse religious and moral educations which, even when furiously rejected, continue to undermine thought and life. Coming from entirely different disciplines, and apparently not wounded by their yoke, R. Schwaller de Lubicz can yet affirm: "If the sense of shame and of the aesthetic must be negated in the erotic, the sense of life and of the sacred cannot be negated without simultaneously provoking the negation of the erotic itself."[18]

Breton never concealed the fact that "of love, [he had only] wanted to know the hours of triumph," clarifying his position thus:

I do not deny that love goes against the grain of life. I say that it must triumph and in order to do that it must be elevated to such a poetic consciousness of itself that everything it encounters which is necessarily hostile to it is grounded on the hearth of its own glory.[19]

And so he goes on to attack the "fearsome sophism,"

which consists in presenting the accomplishment of the sexual act as being necessarily accompanied by a drop in the amorous potential which exists between two beings, a drop whose recurrence will progressively lead them to a point where they will no longer be sufficient to each other. Thus love would be exposing itself to its own destruction as it pursued its own realization.[20]

This passage manifests in a way which is particularly visible to all eyes (or, more exactly, *should* be visible to all eyes, if so much did not serve to obscure it) Breton's irresistible conviction that "real life" must be conquered by a complete remaking of our mental (and even physiological) habits, which would allow us to escape from the "ancient game" of the flesh to the extent that this game merges with a form of resignation, an amorous *vieillerie* (outdatedness, as Rimbaud spoke of a poetic *vieillerie*). There is no doubt that the "vessel of love," its hull, prow and stern redesigned by Breton, sails very far in advance of the courtly tradition as well as of the libertine tradition (of which each perhaps makes up one of its sides), and very far in advance also of the actual state of the "empire of the senses" and of the passions.

To my eyes, nothing demonstrates better the extent of this progress than a re-reading of *Arcane 17*, a book which is not only one of Breton's most remarkable works but is also one of the incomparable jewels among all the books ever written in the French language. It is, certainly, a difficult book; a lyrical current moves through it, mingling the spectacle of nature (the work was written at Perce, on the coast of Gaspesie in Québec, facing Bonaventure Island) and reflections on the historical events which were taking place at the time (20 August–20 October 1944) with a reconsideration of the ideas which had been of fundamental importance to Breton throughout his life. The idea of love, like the others, can be grasped here at its most extreme degree of incandescence. This can be judged from the following fragments taken from a single paragraph:

Setting aside all fallacious and untenable ideas of redemption, it is precisely through love and love alone that the fusion of existence and essence is realized to the highest degree; it is love alone which succeeds in immediately reconciling, in full harmony and without equivocation, these two notions, while outside of love they are always worried and hostile. . . . "Finding the place and the formula" merges with "possessing the truth in a soul and a body"; this supreme aspiration suffices to open out beyond itself the allegorical field which maintains that every human being has been thrown into this life in search of a being of the opposite sex, one only, who will be his match in all respects, to the point where one without the other will appear to be the product of dissociation or dislocation of a single stream of light. . . . In the most general sense, love survives only through reciprocity, which does not at all mean that it is necessarily reciprocal; a much lesser sentiment can, in passing, take pleasure being reflected and even exalted to some extent. But reciprocated love is the only love which provides the conditions of total magnetization, over which nothing can have any hold, and which makes flesh into sunlight, and the flesh's splendid imprint, the spirit, into a spring which gushes forever, inalterable and eternally alive, whose water flows once and for all between the marsh marigolds and the wild thyme.[21]

It is not only love which finds its exaltation here, but also the figure of woman, no longer viewed as a lover, but as the force which is responsible for our destinies, for, Breton writes, at the crucial date of 1944,

the time has come to valorize the ideas of women at the expense of the ideas of men, whose failure is being tumultuously consummated today. It is up to the artist in particular to protest against the scandalous state of things, to make all that comes out of the feminine system of the world predominate in opposition to the masculine system, to base his work on exclusively female properties, to exalt, or better yet, to appropriate and make jealously his own all that distinguishes her from man as far as modes of appreciation and volition are concerned. . . . Art must resolutely give its support to the so-called feminine "irrational," and must hold in fierce enmity anything which has the presumption to present itself as sure, as solid, and thus bears the mark of that masculine intransigeance which, on the level of human and of international relations, is demonstrating today what it is capable of. It is no longer the hour, I say, to restrain ourselves on this point to vague impulses, or to more or less embarrassed concessions; the time has come to pronounce that art is unequivocally against man and on the side of woman, to strip man of a power which he has sufficiently proven that he misuses, and to replace that power in the hands of woman, to strip man of all his authority until such time as woman has succeeded in regaining her fair share of this power, no longer in art, but in life.[22]

I have permitted myself such extensive citations, firstly, because of the continued obscurity in which *Arcane 17* exists, even for the most cultivated public, and, secondly, because of the importance of what is at stake, and, above all, because of the deplorable reception this work has received from the women it was destined for. Yes, it cannot be concealed, women (or rather, certain women who have declared themselves, rightly or wrongly, the spokespeople of their entire sex) have taken *Arcane 17* very badly; they have not welcomed this invitation to seize a power "which [man] has sufficiently proven that he misuses." But because no feminine voice has been raised to take up, in this regard, an alternative discourse, one is inclined to conclude that Breton was mistaken in thinking that it was advisable from then on to "resolutely . . . support the so-called feminine 'irrational,'" that this was, in fact, an intolerably masculine point of view ("macho" or "sexist," as, apparently, they say today!), and that feminine and feminist women had better things to do than busy themselves with making the "feminine system of the world predominate." In truth, the reasons why the ideas formulated by Breton for ending the "infinite servitude of woman" have not yet, that I know of, found a worthy spokeswoman, can be found in *Arcane 17* itself.[23]

25

When he received at Perce the news, with all of its particular exaltation, of the liberation of Paris, Breton nonetheless wrote: "The effort of liberation coincides only partially and fortuitously with the battle for liberty." For

the idea of liberation has against it that it is a negative idea, that it has worth only momentarily and in regards to a clearly defined fact of exploitation which must be forced to cease. Every idea which is not constructive in itself – as, for example, the anti-fascism of the pre-war years, stuck in the rut of pure opposition – is of mediocre scope. The idea of liberty, on the contrary, is an idea which is fully master of itself, which reflects an unconditional view of what *qualifies* man and what alone gives an appreciable sense of human *becoming*. Liberty is not, like liberation, the fight against sickness; liberty is *health*.[24]

These views would soon reveal themselves to be prophetic in post-liberation France. But they were no less prophetic for what we are considering here, that is, the considerable difference of direction between the current movements of "women's liberation" and Breton's perception of female resources for the recuperation of the human spirit of liberty.

In the text on Arnim to which I have already alluded, Breton cites the "physicist, but also cabalist, theosophist and poet" Johann Wilhelm Ritter (1776–1810), who had a strong influence on German Romanticism:

Ritter mysteriously proclaimed that man, a stranger to the earth, can only be acclimated to it by woman. He only "releases" woman; he helps her to discover her purest destiny. It is the earth which, in some way, ordains through woman. "We love only the earth and through woman the earth loves us in return."[25]

But in 1933, Breton continued: "This is why love and women are the clearest solution to all enigmas." And, citing Ritter once more: "Know woman, then all the rest will come of itself."[26] *Beauty can be retained only at this price.*

Translated by Esther Allen

Notes

1. Skira-Flammarion has recently reprinted this magazine in three volumes.

2. André Breton, *La Clé des champs* (Paris: Sagittaire, 1953), 34–35. Reedited by Pauvert.

3. André Breton, *L'Amour fou* (Paris: Gallimard, 1937), 26. Reissued in the "Folio" collection.

4. Ibid., 12–13.

5. Ibid., 115–16.

6. *La Clé des champs,* 99. The italics are Breton's.

7. Ibid., 37.

8. Ibid., 131.

9. Jules Monnerot, *La Poésie moderne et le sacré* (Paris: Gallimard, 1946), 203. The italics are Monnerot's.

10. "Recherches sur la sexualité" in *La Révolution surréaliste* 11 (15 March 1928).

11. Title of the inquiry whose results were published in the twelfth and last issue of *La Révolution surréaliste* (15 December 1929).

12. André Breton, *Point du jour* (Paris: Gallimard, 1934), 188. Reissued in the "Idées" collection.

13. *L'Amour fou,* 108.

14. Ibid., 136.

15. Ibid.

16. "A ce prix," preface to an exhibition by Jean-Claude Silbermann, *Le Surréalisme et la peinture* (Paris: Gallimard, 1965), 407–8.

17. Ibid., 378–79.

18. Ibid., 379–81.

19. *L'Amour fou,* 172.

20. Ibid., 134.

21. André Breton, *Arcane 17* (Paris: Sagittaire, 1947), 38–41. Reissued by Pauvert and 10/18.

22. Ibid., 87–90.

23. The case of Annie Le Brun cannot be completely exemplary since she participated in the activities of the surrealist movement during Breton's lifetime. On the other hand, I admit that I expect a great deal in this respect from someone like Claire Lejeune and from the *serenity* of her regard.

24. *Arcane 17,* 166–67.

25. *Point du jour,* 189.

26. Ibid.

Breton and Poetic Originality
Stamos Metzidakis

As startling and unpredictable as most surrealist images may be, it would be a gross error to think that the writers who created them were any more concerned with originality than other modern writers have been. Indeed, for the last two hundred years or so, poets in particular and artists in general have tried assiduously to create forms and to express feelings that in some fashion or other differ from those of their predecessors.[1] To a large extent, this modus operandi in the aesthetic domain seems so obvious, so "natural" (especially in modern critical circles), that to doubt its feasibility or desirability constitutes a major affront to contemporary sensibilities. That is, nearly everyone seems to think it reasonable, if not also "good" in some quasi-moral or transcendental way, that poets continually seek to be original in style, thought, and emotion whenever they set out to write their next work.

Such a positive view of originality's role, however, has not always enjoyed the same popularity among all groups of readers and writers. If we single out French poets, we cannot help but note how much of their practice – from various medieval borrowings of Latin rhetorical devices to the general acceptance of generic conventions in the majority of eighteenth-century poetry – reflects a somewhat different attitude vis-à-vis writers and their traditional tasks qua writers. Specifically, what these practices make clear is that, during a period of nearly a thousand years, poets in France were assumed to have a kind of moral and aesthetic debt to pay to certain all-important precursors. Their responsibility consisted essentially in maintaining the quasi-imperial power and prestige of these "classic" models through a dutiful and respectful copying (*translatio*) of them. The traditional approach to the writing of poetry was thus limited, more or less, to a proper imitation of the great poets and poems of what T. S. Eliot, in an English context, called The Tradition.

This does not mean, of course, that prior to the nineteenth century no one ever sought to write a *really* new or original poem. The whole debate in France between the so-called *Modernes et Anciens*, for example, which lasted for more than 150 years, centered precisely on this question of choosing between old styles and past wisdom, and something more up to date. The Pléiade poets too, in their strong defense of the French language, were obviously firmly committed to the idea of writing poetry that in some ways, at least, would go beyond the Italian, Greek, and Roman models they used. But, as Roland Mortier has demonstrated recently, these longstanding debates were resolved for all intents and purposes around the end of the eighteenth century, with a resounding victory for the Moderns.[2] In essence, what Mortier contends is that with the advent of Romantic literary theory in England, Germany, and France, the concept of *originality* in and of itself became a distinct aesthetic category or criterion for both the creation and appreciation of literary works. Whereas the quest for a certain distinctiveness had, to be sure, always tempted poets, Mortier argues that this search gradually became a veritable obsession with the Romantics.

Now if we consider Surrealism, as have many before us, to be the twentieth-century parallel to Romanticism, it would seem extremely useful (within the context of a more comprehensive theory of originality's place in modern literary criticism) to examine André Breton's particular conception of it. How does Breton define his own poetic originality? What do his ideas on the subject tell us about the role Surrealism plays in the history of this important notion? First of all, it must be stated that from his earliest writings on, Breton wanted to make clear the distance he wished to establish from those individuals he disdainfully called "poets." As he says in *Les Pas perdus,* "Were it not for him [his friend Jacques Vaché], I probably would have been a poet."[3] This suggests that from Breton's perspective no true "spirit of his time" would ever deign to write in a manner that, over the years, his contemporaries had come to assume was in some shape or form standard operating poetic procedure. No self-respecting artist who worked with and in the medium of written words could help, therefore, "losing his neighbors" (*égarer ses voisins, PP,* 14) in the course of his creative act. If one truly wanted to "progress" as an intellectual or *"bel esprit"* one would be well advised, from this point of view, to cease thinking idealistically of the activity known as writing.

Accordingly, the sole progress possible in the literary domain can occur only upon first challenging what Breton refers to as "written poetry" (*la poésie écrite*), that is, that conventional type of composition dear to the vast majority of earlier scriptural artists. Breton was convinced that most older approaches to poetic creation were inappropriate for his generation and society; that they had to be replaced by a practice that would no longer produce "mere" literature. (One thinks here of Verlaine's analogous scorn for *tout le reste.*) In any case, the practice as conceived by Breton had only begun to be exploited by certain writers in the second half of the nineteenth century, the most important being Ducasse, Rimbaud, and Germain Nouveau: "Written poetry is losing its very reason-for-being day after day . . . these [earlier] authors never made a profession out of writing" (*PP,* 115). His wish to eliminate conventional writing practices explains also, no doubt, why Breton greatly admired Apollinaire's expressed goal of the "reinvention of poetry."

The progress he had in mind cannot be understood, therefore, except in terms of a more general human movement towards a better condition, a more complete and satisfying existence. His desire to fuse philosophy and poetry with life itself recalls Socratic and Platonic ideals. Given his respect for the nineteenth-century utopian thinker Charles Fourier, this kind of philanthropic, idealistic underpinning is evident throughout his work. As a result, what we need to emphasize from the start of our examination is how intimately linked for him are the values of poetic originality and human progress. His most important artistic consideration lies in the catalytic power of images in surrealist poetry to help society's members learn more about themselves and each other. If the products of his espoused automatic writing technique do not lead him and/or his readers to the eventual formulation of a "collective myth," their *originality* has served no real purpose. Breton's notion of a collective myth is analogous to the "modern mythology" which Aragon sought to record in *Le Paysan de Paris* by collecting various poetic *trouvailles* in the course of real and imagined "aleatory movements." It includes all those archetypal forms which a given society discovers, produces, preserves, and admires in order to foster among its members a sense of community and social identity.

Yet, once again, the new lyricism he promotes differs formally from that of earlier "writers." Citing Robert Desnos's hypnotic trances as a case in point, he states that "it seems to me certain . . . that the new lyricism will find the means of *translating* itself without the help of books" (*PP*, 174). Thus, poetry is useful to men and women when it avoids giving them false hope in the infallibly positive value of any and all scientific progress. On the contrary, science is beneficial only if it brings us closer to nature:

The scientific study of nature has no value except on the condition that *contact* with nature through poetic and, I daresay, mythical channels be reestablished. It remains clear that any scientific progress accomplished within the framework of a defective social structure only works against Man, and serves to aggravate his condition. This was already the opinion shared by Fontenelle.[4]

Here Breton alludes to an earlier Golden Age of Nature, a primordial state of bliss in which opposites, incarnated by the quintessential figure of the Androgyne, were fused. Recovering this anterior state of existential union becomes the single most significant purpose for his writing, since this recovery inevitably results from the "state of grace" with which any bona fide surrealist poet is occasionally "blessed," as it were. In the often-quoted beginning of his *Second Manifesto*, the mental place (*lieu mental*) he comes to inhabit while in the trance-like state of automatic writing becomes, in Breton's words, the "culminating point" or "supreme point" of human existence itself. In this place, all opposites "cease to be perceived contradictorily," and reunite as one.

The emotional and cognitive rewards of this mystical reunion were so great to Breton's thinking that whatever poetic originality he may have exhibited has to be evaluated – within the context of his own thought – in direct proportion to his success or failure in restoring the "eidetic image" of this original state. For him, the discoveries of automatic writing help us better to understand why the modern separation of direct perception of objects, and their subsequent re-presentation, are but unfortunate accidents. These accidents are the result of our having somehow forgotten an earlier, more unified mind-set. Automatic writing lets us capture traces of this mind-set almost effortlessly. Much about the nature of this imagined, childlike, antediluvian world to which Breton, metaphorically, would have us try to return (one which, incidentally, recalls the newly cleansed world of Rimbaud's prose poem, "Après le déluge"), can be discovered by studying remnants or traces of this holistic state in specific privileged individuals:

All of the experimentation now undertaken would be of a nature to demonstrate that perception and representation – which seem to the ordinary adult to be so radically opposed to one another – must be considered merely as the products of dissociations from a unique, original faculty . . . of which traces can be found in primitive people and children.[5]

Throughout his works we find this idea of a perceptual and emotional reunion which Surrealism aspired to bring about, one that would result "from the conciliation *into one lone being . . . of everything that can be expected from the outside and the inside.*"[6] The crucial point for Breton, however, is that this universe has always been there, well before modern art and science came along to fragment it into separate domains. Though it was not created *ex nihilo,* it has remained hidden nevertheless to most people since the beginning of history. One of the most original goals of surrealist poetry was precisely to learn how to read the present world as if it were a "cryptogram" or, in other words, "to recover the secret of a language whose elements ceased to behave [merely] like ship-wrecks on the surface of a dead sea."[7] To accomplish this, it was necessary to avoid putting words to what he calls a "strictly utilitarian" usage. Only in this manner would one be able to emancipate words, and to give back to them the power they supposedly had in an earlier era. When we talk about originality in Breton's scheme of things, we are not talking, therefore, about the merits of individual *poets* who create, control, or manipulate something new. Rather we refer to the inherent value of any and all deliberate attempts to let loose this same *something* to which, failing a better term, we give the name "poetry."

Louis Aragon makes a similar point in his *Traité du style* (1928) with respect to Surrealism itself. In that text, the latter is defined as "recognized, accepted, and practiced inspiration. Not as an inexplicable visitation, but as a faculty that is practiced."[8] What Aragon shares with Breton – and we might add Mallarmé as well – is the belief that words have so much intrinsic beauty and force that ultimately they reduce the poet's role to a most mechanical one indeed. Writers who lack genuine talent will, of course, continue to hope that their poems exhibit a certain originality when they are read by the public. The least-talented writers believe that the individual differences their works bring to the body of literature are, by definition, original traits that are worthy of the reader's respect and admiration.

In the final analysis, poetic originality as Breton understands it really only matters when one becomes adept at transcribing particularly powerful, albeit fortuitous, lexical sequences. The original poet, to be sure, has a feel for the emotive power (Reverdy) of certain lexical encounters. But he also acts vigilantly to manipulate and arrange them in such a way as to bring about a kind of poetic explosion of meaning and form. In the end, these sequences of words alone are the entities which "make love" to each other in the text, to borrow Breton's phrase. The discovery of original images thus constitutes the most important task of the poet who sits down in a comfortable place, as Breton advises in the "Secrets de l'art magique sur-réaliste" section of his *Manifesto,* and begins to write rapidly, without preconceptions. It is no doubt significant that the word "origin" reappears in this same section, where Breton advises the poet to reject any word "whose *origin* seems suspect" [my emphasis]. What he seems to be suggesting here is that "true" originality has much to do with a specific, that is, correct *origin.*

The problem of differentiating between "valuable" and worthless transcriptions of what thought dictates remains a serious one. For Breton and many others it remained a kind of theoretical thorn in their critical side. To see how annoying a problem this was, we find a very telling remark in the same passage from Aragon's *Traité du style* quoted above. While stressing the need for energy in the exercise of what Breton called one's "original faculty," Aragon admits that the results of automatic writing are "of an unequal interest." In other words, while all surrealist images are created equal in principle, practically speaking they are not all equal.

Here again, Breton's particular conception of poetic originality helps us to resolve another apparent enigma. Let us recall first the reason why he chose not to publish many of the poems he and his friends wrote. In his *Second Manifesto,* he reveals a major objection to these texts. He states that they kept the poet (and, presumably, the reader) "as uninformed as always about the *origin* of that *voice* that it behooves everyone to hear"[9] [my emphasis]. I have stressed the word "origin" in the last quotation in order to reemphasize the peculiar nature of the Surrealist's quest. For in this example and others we have already seen, we are confronted with an extraordinary situation in which the ultimate index of a poem's *originality,* in Breton's perspective, lies in its dual capacity to return both writer and reader to a particular mental place or *origin*. It would appear, then, that the supreme or culminating point of the mind alluded to earlier is simultaneously the point of departure *and* of destination for surrealist poetry. Insofar as the former point is the location where, precisely, opposites are no longer supposed to be perceived as such, there is moreover a certain consistency in our fusing these apparently different points. What makes one automatic poem "better" than another, therefore, is that the first exhibits more *origin*ality than the second, that is, it comes closer to conjuring up the common mental place from which a sacred, quasi-redemptive inner voice *origin*ates in us all.

As unsatisfying as this formal aesthetic criterion may seem, it is surely much less so than Aragon's, as set forth in the abovementioned paragraph of *Traité du style*. Reminiscent of Reverdy's formulation of the poetic image (which, we recall, combined "emotive power and poetic reality"), it too stressed the idea that a "good" poem exhibits both "strength and novelty." In addition to these rather vague, intangible qualities, Aragon cites still another aspect of the so-called valuable automatic text, which he describes in even more problematic fashion. He says simply that such poems are "well written," and that "writing well is like walking straight." In the wake of Formalism, New Criticism, and Structuralism, it is practically impossible to overemphasize the uselessness of this comparison. Whereas it pretends to explicate a phenomenon by means of a common sense reference to the ordinary action of walking, it merely increases our confusion by calling into question the notion of doing anything whatsoever *well*.[10] Exactly how does writing resemble walking? Better yet, in which precise ways can we presume to say even figuratively that one writes as if he or she were stumbling instead of walking *straight?*

Clearly, what results from this interrogation is that *no* definitive formal guiding principle exists for differentiating among good, bad, and ugly automatic poems. The final "judge" of quality in this, and so many other matters involving surrealist practice, thus had to be Breton himself, much to the ultimate chagrin of most of his earliest collaborators. I do not mean to suggest that his fellow poets did not or could not determine better than he which poems were somehow superior to others. I am merely trying to stress that, given his unshakable faith in the intrinsic value of the mental origin of the surrealist voice, he could accept as truly original only those contemporary poems which best manifested his *personal* vision of this psychic point, or of what we might call the original image-reservoir of all thought and writing.

The term "originality" in Breton's work—which, incidentally, does not appear often, if at all, in its nominal form—acts, therefore, much like the rhetorical trope of syllepsis.[11] This is to say that, as with any other instance of syllepsis, it enters into different kinds of semantic relations with the words in his *oeuvre*. One could even say that it has different meanings inasmuch as it signifies figuratively *and* literally in the same instance. For, on the one hand, "original" images are valorized because they have presumably never before appeared in the course of literary history. Their newness breathes fresh life thereby into the tired world of written poetry. On the other hand, what really makes them original for Breton is their configurational propinquity to that unspeakable, unsayable origin of thought to which the Surrealists tried to remain attentive. This origin cannot be articulated but merely alluded to, for it is precisely that psychic source which gives rise to all other (poetic) saying.

It should be mentioned in passing, at least, that Breton hesitates even to qualify as "thought" the *thing* which derives from this inner source of inspiration. Let us consider, for example, the following sentence we read in one of his very last texts, entitled *Le La* (1960):

The "dictation of thought" (or of something else?) to which Surrealism wanted to submit itself *originally* ["*originellement*," my emphasis], and on which it wanted to rely through so-called "automatic writing," to how very many risks in waking life have I said its audition (active-passive) is exposed.[12]

In this passage, one can clearly appreciate the potential double meaning of the word "originality" as we attribute it to Breton. Thus, while Surrealism's most striking innovation was, to be sure, its reliance on a new type of writing, the latter's most important dimension lay in its capacity to return both writer and reader to a (the?) unified u-topia, or "supreme point."

A final comment on *Le La* needs to be made since it is absolutely germane to the question at hand. Breton admits that Victor Hugo's "Bouche d'ombre" never spoke to him the same way, nor even to the same extent, as it did to the great earlier poet. Yet, the only thing that appears essential for Breton in this regard is that this same mouth/voice spoke to him *on occasion (parfois)*. The words it proffered, he insists, were addressed to him alone (*à moi seul*). He knew this to be the case because he perceived a distinct similarity between this other voice and his own. These remarks remind us how the idea of originality in Breton's conceptual framework has two different sides. A few words whispered to him *personally* would end up forming the structure of a kind of "collective" poem he said was the one he cherished most throughout his life. The title he chose for the poem, "Les Etats généraux," evokes perhaps the most *collective* act of creation in French history, the making of the Republic itself. The allusion to this quintessentially collective act, however, serves as the title to what Breton would have had us believe was a poem whispered to him alone. (In reality, Breton first heard a simple one-sentence image, "There will always be a shovel in the sands of dreams," that he then segmented in such a way as to form a much longer poem, much in the same fashion as Mallarmé did with his *Coup de dés*.)

34

Thus, while he loved "Les Etats généraux" because of the specific "personalized" phrase/image which inspired him to write it, he used the image as a pretext for a more elaborate poetic reinvocation of a longstanding wish. As we saw earlier, his wish was for a new "collective myth" in which everyone could partake and participate. The desire to be an original poet therefore never prevented Breton from keeping a social sense about the goals he set forth for his artistic and political practice. In other words, he never wanted to be merely an original poet. His real ambition was to become an original *thinker*. If we consider his texts original, then they are so not as a result of their "mere" literary re-presentation of what Apollinaire first called "surreality." Their ultimate specificity consists instead in a singular *presentation* of a different reality, a more holistic, anterior existence. As Breton says at the end of the *First Manifesto:* "Existence is elsewhere." To express this idea as Laurent Jenny has, we might also say that "the originality of [Breton's] textual organization is not a *sign* of surreality, it *is* its surreality itself."[13]

Notes

1. To this group I might also add *critics,* whose ever-varying interpretations of the same canonical works make it clear that they, too, are anxious to be original somehow, and in their own fashion, regardless of the relative worth of their different hermeneutic methodologies or conclusions.

2. See Roland Mortier, *L'Originalité: une nouvelle catégorie esthétique au siècle des lumières* (Geneva: Droz, 1982).

3. André Breton, *Les Pas perdus* (Paris: Gallimard, 1969), 9. This, and all other passages from the French, are my own translations. Further references to this collection of essays by Breton are incorporated in the text, followed by *PP* and the page number.

4. André Breton, *Entretiens* (Paris: Gallimard, 1973), 251–52.

5. André Breton, *Point du jour* (Paris: Gallimard, 1970), 188.

6. André Breton, *Arcane 17* (Paris: U.G.E., 1965), 147–48.

7. André Breton, *Du Surréalisme en ses oeuvres vives* (1953), in his *Manifestes du surréalisme* (Paris: Jean Jacques Pauvert, 1962), 311.

8. Louis Aragon, *Traité du style* (Paris: Gallimard, 1980), 187–89.

9. In Breton, *Manifestes,* 163.

10. In order to avoid any misunderstanding of my point here, I should indicate that in the original French Aragon uses the adverb *"bien"* in the context of both statements: (1) a poem *"bien écrit,"* and (2) writing well, *"bien écrire."*

11. See Michael Riffaterre's extensive work on this trope, especially his article "Syllepsis," *Critical Inquiry* 6 (Summer 1980), 625–38.

12. In André Breton, *Signe ascendant* (Paris: Gallimard, 1968), 174.

13. Laurent Jenny, "La Surréalité et ses signes narratifs," *Poétique* 4 (1973), 520.

André Breton and Painting: The Case of Arshile Gorky

J. H. Matthews

An assertion by William S. Rubin – that Arshile Gorky, a Turkish Armenian raised in the United States, was "the last major painter to be associated with the surrealist movement" – has gone unchallenged in the United States.[1] Whether or not we ponder Rubin's use of the adjective "major," his "cultural cannibalism" – as one Surrealist, José Pierre, calls it[2] – need detain us for one reason only. Treating Gorky as the singer of Surrealism's swan song, Rubin arbitrarily terminates the history of surrealist painting in 1947. He then goes on to present Gorky's work as linking Surrealism with American Abstract Expressionism. In other words, he attempts to locate discussion of both Surrealism and Gorky on the plane of aesthetics, where no surrealist artist would look for or admit evaluation of his or her efforts.

So far as Rubin detects and acknowledges points of contact between Gorky and the surrealist movement, he places the latter within a tradition of painterly forms. In doing so, he appreciates best what his acquaintance with tradition enables him to grasp. At the same time, however, he fails to respond to essential features of Surrealism that are necessarily and profoundly antitraditional. Hence the acid tone adopted by José Pierre: "I mean that when the honorable curator stops talking painting (and sculpture), his competence would cease to dazzle even a reader of *France-Soir.*" Pierre proceeds to wonder "why William put himself in the position of speaking of movements that, no more the one than the other, can be reduced to the plastic arts alone."

José Pierre's harshness is self-evident. Less obvious, perhaps, is that he is harsh for reasons of principle, not out of pique or animosity. To appreciate his position as a Surrealist, we have to comprehend the significance of his reference to Rubin as "talking painting," and we need to understand concurrently the fundamental importance of the inference his readers are invited to draw: dealing with Surrealism does not mean talking either painting or sculpture after the manner of art critics. The approach adopted by Pierre suggests that speaking productively of Surrealism is neither the occasion nor the permissible excuse for talking the aesthetics of painting.

36

All this, we notice, sounds distinctly advantageous to the advocates of Surrealism. It looks as though Surrealism has withdrawn safely outside criticism only because it has been carried out of range by defenders presumably intent on cutting off any objection before it is even put into words. Yet Surrealism is far from being a movement founded on self-indulgence and raised in self-congratulation. A surrealist artist does not seek to ward off criticism by the convenient expedient of denying its relevance. Instead, he rejects criticism that aims to weigh his achievement by standards he has no wish at all to meet, because he finds them entirely valueless. As Pierre indicates, Surrealists object to judgment by anyone whose terms of reference exclude the ones by which they have been working and by which they consider they have every right to expect evaluations to be made.

Here we see what is at issue when Surrealists scoff at professional critics of art, and the latter, in their turn, voice skepticism about Surrealism's accomplishment in the medium of painting. It would be easy to conclude in favor of the Surrealists, if critics could be proved guilty of blind prejudice. On the other hand, one would have no qualms about siding with unaffiliated commentators if their criteria could be seen as condemning surrealist values beyond appeal, as revealing them to be unworthy of serious consideration. Looking at William S. Rubin's comments in *Dada and Surrealist Art,* though, we have a foretaste of the complexity of the situation. Rubin denies the right claimed by all Surrealists and does so in an interestingly roundabout fashion that might well have been designed to discredit Surrealism.

Reviewing how André Breton wrote about painters he loved, Rubin suggests that Breton identified so completely with those men and women that he "rarely found it possible to speak of their shortcomings (if and when he was at all aware of them)."[3] Remarking that Breton's writing "deals more with painters than with painting" – as indeed it most significantly does – Rubin pronounces it so personal, so "lyrically effusive," that its author's "occasional remarks about the works themselves remain obscure."

André Breton is being attacked from two sides at once, though for one and the same crime. Because he "rarely addressed himself to the formal aspects of painting" in this or that artist's work, he was, according to Rubin, unquestionably indifferent to the weakness of formal features. Meanwhile, since he "remained almost totally involved in the *subject* of the picture," Breton's discussion thereof is to be rejected as "obscure."

Against attacks of which Rubin's strictures are representative, participants in the surrealist venture have uniformly defended themselves with too much vigor. All the same, a reminder of the divergence of opinion that sets the art critic at a substantial distance from the Surrealist is useful at this stage. It helps to show why, to Breton, whose vantage point was Surrealism, the work of Arshile Gorky looked decidedly different from the way it looks to the aesthetician of painting.

In one important respect, Gorky stands out from the painters whose names come most quickly to mind when Surrealism is mentioned. This was no neophyte, eagerly seeking his way, for whom the blandishments of Surrealism were to prove irresistible. Gorky's art had already taken a definite course and had assumed some individuality before circumstances – the exile of several Surrealists, including André Breton, who found themselves in New York at one time or another during the Second World War – brought him close to Surrealism. Also, by the time Gorky made the discovery of Surrealism, the latter could boast a sizable number of adherents who had made a mark on recent painting. In Gorky's eyes, then, Surrealism was much more than an exotic European phenomenon. It was a noteworthy import to which major painters (Max Ernst, André Masson, and Yves Tanguy were now on American soil) had been willing to lend both name and reputation. Gorky, for his part, was not pressed into surrealist service.

Essential details remain blurred unless we consider what interested Breton in Gorky's work and what, in return, Gorky derived from contact with Surrealism and, eventually, with Breton himself.

Arshile Gorky's formation as an artist was entirely respectable, and for this very reason looked quite suspect to the Surrealists, at first. From the time he arrived on the American continent at the age of fifteen, in 1920, until he changed his name from Vosdanig Adoian in 1925, he had painted still lifes and portraits after the example of Cézanne. There followed a five-year period during which he worked under the influence of Cubism. And he took inspiration from Pablo Picasso, too, not to mention Wassily Kandinsky. However, even while looking upon Gorky as "a typical hero of Abstract Expressionism," Harold Rosenberg admits that "it was the shift of his verbal consciousness into the formulas of psychological experiments and magic brought to these shores by the Surrealists at the beginning of World War II that released Gorky's hand for the radical creation of the final period."[4] Rosenberg's idea of Surrealism is a little fanciful. All the same, he lets credit fall where it is due.

André Breton had arrived in New York, via Martinique and Santo Domingo, in the latter half of 1941, when Ernst and Masson also arrived. Yet he and Gorky did not meet until 1944. Their encounter prompted a familiar gesture of cordiality from Breton. In January 1945 he prefaced the catalogue of a Gorky show with a text added to the New York edition of his *Le Surréalisme et la peinture*, published in April of the same year.

While meeting Breton may have been decisive in Gorky's final alignment with Surrealism, it actually did no more than allow the artist to complete a step well prepared in advance. Surely Edward Henning is quite correct in asserting that "Gorky's confidence in his art was reinforced by Breton's friendship."[5] This is not to say that, natural and unforced as it was, Gorky's evolution toward Surrealism took place completely without penalty. His devotion to a number of masters – Cézanne at the top of the list – proved to be an impediment in one important respect. It gave his work a quality of line much admired in critical circles. Concurrently, it denied him, for example, the ability to respond without reservation to graphic automatism, as advocated and practiced by his friend Matta Echaurren. Thus we cannot comprehend the nature of Gorky's relationship with Surrealism without appreciating one factor: although Surrealism opened the door on perspectives he was more than willing to contemplate, it did not guarantee Arshile Gorky ready access to them. In some ways, his advance into the realm of the surreal was seriously hampered by his education in art. Even so, the consequence was not disappointing failure to attain surrealist goals. What happened was that he found it necessary to approach Surrealism by paths of his own. That he managed to do so in a distinctly original fashion explains André Breton's keen interest in his work and admiration for virtues peculiar to it.

When the occasion presented itself to comment publicly on Gorky's art, Breton elected to emphasize, first, the painter's eye. He wrote, "I say that the eye is not *open* so long as it limits itself to the passive role of mirror . . . – that this eye has the effect on me of being no less dead than that of a felled bullock if it shows itself capable only of *reflecting*."[6] Breton now affirmed that the eye's "treasure" lies elsewhere. Nevertheless, he argued, most artists are still at the stage of turning the watch face in all directions (the metaphor is his) without having the faintest idea of the spring hidden inside. Therefore Gorky's distinction, as Breton perceived it, was that of being the first painter to unveil, completely, "the eye's spring."[7]

The perspective in which Breton looked at Gorky's work is illuminating. It indicates rejection of the view that the painter's eye serves to "inventorize like a bailiff's." More important still, it sets Arshile Gorky apart from the madman, whose eye "takes pleasure in illusions of false reconnaissance," as Breton put it. With uncompromising dismissal of artists whose aim is confined to recording the visible goes also unqualified disapproval of those whose work bears witness to their total withdrawal from reality. And so Breton located Gorky's place, as a Surrealist, somewhere between the two groups. Here Gorky's painting demonstrates the possibility of *using* the real, without paying the unacceptable price of falling victim to it.

Elaborating upon this last thought led Breton to revert to an image he had developed several years earlier. He spoke now of the eye as being suited to "making a *conducting thread* pass between things of most heterogeneous aspect." That is to say, he took up again in his observations about the painter's eye the theme of communication between reality and dream, between the concrete and the imagined, that is central to a book he published in 1932, *Les Vases communicants.*

From the standpoint of Surrealism, Breton's enthusiasm for Gorky's work was not simply legitimate; it was only to be expected. Expressing his belief that the conducting thread to which he had referred permits apprehension of the (surreal) relationship linking innumerable physical and mental structures, André Breton arrived at a statement climaxing in a word having paramount importance in surrealist thought governing all forms of creative action, painting included: "The key to the mental prison can be found only by breaking with these ridiculous means of knowing: it resides in the free and unlimited play of *analogies.*"[8]

Analogical play never ceases to be one of the major seminal aspects of Surrealism. It is a centrally characteristic feature of creative activity common to painters and writers alike. It denotes their shared ambition to acquire a mode of communication that will transcend the mundane, surpassing the real in the attainment of the surreal. André Breton could have paid an artist, regardless of his or her medium, no greater tribute than he offered when commending Arshile Gorky for applying the analogical principle successfully. Therefore we could not ask for a more revealing difference than the one that comes to light as soon as Breton's comments on a famous Gorky canvas are placed next to Rubin's assessment of the same picture.

Rubin sees *The Liver Is the Cock's Comb* (1944) as "a synthesis, in an entirely personal form, of the painterly language inspired by Kandinsky, the biomorphism of Miró, and the automatic surreal 'Inscape' of Matta."[9] The point of view bestowing meaning and value on these phrases is that of the art critic. The perspective from which Rubin traces the derivation of Gorky's "painterly language," meanwhile, is that of the art historian. *The Liver Is the Cock's Comb* survives scrutiny in *Dada and Surrealist Art* to stand, finally, among "Gorky's most stunning canvases." This picture, we are informed, "contains some remarkable passages and recommends itself by its ambitiousness." For all that, Rubin is not entirely pleased with it. He labels it "confused and overcrowded in spots," without commenting on the nature of the confusion or pinpointing the "spots." In the end, his objection is that *The Liver Is the Cock's Comb* lacks "the distilling perfection" of certain later Gorky paintings.

Linking perfection with distillation in this manner really links it with confection. Rubin unmasks the standards by which he measures Gorky's use of "great plumes of color," finding these "potentially seductive even though as a group their registration does not cohere." One can see, now, that Rubin intends to address himself to "the general design" of the can-

Arshile Gorky, *The Liver Is the Cock's Comb.* 1944. Oil on canvas, 73¼ × 98 in. Albright-Knox Art Gallery, Buffalo, New York.

vas, regarding this as supremely important, the very focal point of critical attention, in fact. Given the nature of his interest in *The Liver Is the Cock's Comb,* it is no surprise to hear him deal only perfunctorily with an aspect of Gorky's canvas which he calls its "poetry." He grants that this poetry is "comprehensive," then labels it "self-conscious" before declaring that it "must certainly be attributed to Gorky's new contact with the Surrealists." As for the text in which, so he says, Arshile Gorky "describes" *The Liver Is the Cock's Comb,* this strikes him as quite simply "pretentious." After all, he assures his readers, "As with the Surrealists (who suggested many of Gorky's titles), neither Gorky's title nor his description should be taken literally."

We are left between frustration and amusement after hearing a commentator deride an artist's interpretation with such confidence while never entertaining the thought, apparently, that the remarks he himself has to offer in its place may sound as pretentious as Gorky's own words, which run, "The song of a cardinal, liver, mirrors that have not caught reflection, the aggressively heraldic branches, the saliva of the hungry man whose face is painted with white chalk."[10] Breton, for his part, refrains from citing Gorky's words and also from discussing his punning title. This does not necessarily mean that he finds it to his best advantage to ignore what the painter has said. Breton's observations certainly betray no strain

41

such as Rubin's do. Their author appears to have had no difficulty responding to the artist's remarks; they aim higher than an itemization of contents easy to identify in the picture. And there is a reason for this.

During the nineteenth century Charles Fourier was delighted to discover in the cabbage an emblem of mysterious love; he foresaw the establishment of a scale of colors that would make it possible to ascertain for sure "to which passion an animal, vegetable or mineral hieroglyph is linked." Reminding his audience that the range of analogies has been broadly extended since Fourier's day and at the same time refined, André Breton mentions in *Le Surréalisme et la peinture* both Arthur Rimbaud and Lautréamont. Although he does not even begin to comment on the work of these writers, it is only after citing their names that he speaks of *The Liver Is the Cock's Comb*. Gorky's painting, he affirms, "may be considered the great door open upon the *analogical world*."[11]

In view of the admiration for Rimbaud and Lautréamont shared by Breton and other Surrealists, and given the fact that the year he prefaced Gorky's catalogue was the year Breton wrote his *Ode à Charles Fourier*, one might argue, as numerous critics do when commenting on Breton's ideas about painting, that they are "literary." However, the surrealist leader's response would be that he is not alluding to literature (of which every Surrealist remains suspicious) but to a poetic ambition common to Surrealists everywhere, whatever their chosen mode of expression.

Technique receives attention in Surrealism only so far as its utilization promotes the emergence of poetry. By poetry, it should be noted, Breton understood the revelation of relationships of an unprecedented nature, having the virtue of transcending mundane reality. His particular interest in analogy was stimulated, therefore, by its capacity to make connections that, like the one by which the cabbage is transformed into an emblem of love, comes to light in defiance of commonplace (that is to say, commonsense) linkage.

Rubin's analysis sets up a contrast between the literal and the ambiguous. His remarks hint that there is something reprehensible about the latter and something regrettable about the limited use Gorky has made of literal forms: "In *The Liver Is the Cock's Comb* male and female genitalia . . . are the only literal forms to emerge from the otherwise ambiguous context of shapes."[12] Meanwhile, as though anticipating Rubin's later objections, Breton wrote in 1945, "Lovers of facile solutions will get nothing here for their small pains: against all forewarning they will persist in wanting to bring out in these compositions a still life, a landscape and a figure, for lack of daring to face these *hybrid* forms in which all human emotion tends to be precipitated."[13] Breton went on to explain that "hybrids" derive from "contemplation of a natural spectacle coming to terms with the flow of childhood and other memories" that result from extreme concentration by an observer "equipped, to the most exceptional degree, with the gift of emotion." Hence the following pronouncement, apropos of Gorky: "It is no longer a question, with him, of taking the expression of that nature for an *end* but rather of demanding of her sensations capable of acting like *spring-boards* to the deepening, as much in consciousness as in pleasure, of certain states of mind."

Breton concentrates on an aspect of *The Liver Is the Cock's Comb* that he deems essential to Gorky's art. For it is not merely attentiveness to external reality that he finds admirable in Gorky's later work. What he appreciates most is Gorky's gift for suggesting, by way of ambient reality, states of mind that could not have been communicated graphically unless the analogical principle had been brought into play. The issue, then, is not André Breton's incapacity as a critic to measure up to standards in which practitioners of art criticism demonstrate their belief. It is his conviction that attention to these criteria is woefully distracting because it does not take us to the core of the experience for which he himself feels indebted to Arshile Gorky.

Being content with classifying certain motifs – or with persuading ourselves that such motifs are indeed present, because we imagine we recognize them – leads to a very limited form of enjoyment, as we contemplate a Gorky canvas. In the long term or the short, it encourages assessment of the pictorial image on the elementary basis of its supposed or admissible fidelity to objective reality. In this sense, the painting is a success just so far as it seems to accomplish a purpose that can be grasped without undue effort. The trouble is this: the purpose we now ascribe to the painter actually contradicts the aim to which – Breton takes the deepest satisfaction in noticing – Arshile Gorky dedicated himself in his last years.

In no way impaired by the fact that Breton and Gorky did not share a common language, their association persuaded the former that he was putting his finger on Gorky's true intent, in a text that the artist gladly used in the catalogue of his 1945 exhibition. Breton felt sure he was bringing Gorky's purpose to light when referring to states of mind for which the sensations demanded of nature are but *"spring-boards,"* when he spoke of these states as sharing, in their formulation, "the sublime difficulty that spring flowers have in emerging to the light." Drawing his analogy very simply, Breton emphasized once again in Gorky's painting the analogical rather than the literal function of phenomena borrowed from the natural world. We are reminded, now, of the Surrealists' abiding respect for Charles Baudelaire as we hear Breton declare that, in Gorky's work, "for the first time nature is treated . . . after the fashion of a cryptogram on which the artist's previous sensitive imprints come to press their *screen,* upon discovery of the very rhythm of life."

At first glance, it may look as though these words fully validate Rubin's contention that André Breton lapsed into obscurity when commenting on painters who met with his approval. Granted, at this juncture Breton's prose is undeniably dense, sinking its roots into a cultural base with which not all his readers are thoroughly acquainted. As difficult as his writing may be, it is not obscurantist. In fact, it allows him to move forward consistently toward the conclusion in which his tribute to Arshile Gorky will culminate. Breton's immediate concern is neither confused nor calculated to sow confusion. Far from shirking his responsibility to bring out the qualities of Gorky's later work, he points directly to the major importance he attributes to it: "For this is an entirely new art, at the opposite pole from everything that, with the aid of fashion and confusion, tends today to simulate Surrealism by confining itself to counterfeiting its procedures from the outside."

André Breton stressed the originality of Gorky's art as defying stereotypes, against which the Surrealists had been warned, no later than 1924, in the *Manifeste du surréalisme.* This is to say that the prospect of finding in Gorky's later painting a solution to this or that technical problem which, subsequently, Abstract Expressionists will feel grateful that he has confronted – or, for that matter, of witnessing the emergence of some "general design" in this or that picture – meant absolutely nothing to Breton. All the same, looking at certain canvases filled him with delight because he saw in them proof that Gorky possessed a "key to the mental prison" restricting our powers of cognition. Neither fashion nor confusion could present a tolerable substitute for such a key, the prison bars being, as Breton pointed out in another context, "on the inside of the cage." At the same time, counterfeiting – the mere imitation of an approach that is immediately disqualified in surrealist eyes, when it comes down to nothing more than a derivative technique – could never succeed in unlocking the mental prison from which Breton looked to creative artists to help us escape.

It is helpful to recall that André Breton condemned social realism as yet one more "imposture" to be laid at the door of a political regime which he accused of "alienating human liberty," among other things. The title of the essay in which he voiced his protest says it all: "Du 'réalisme socialiste' comme moyen d'extermination morale."[14] The freedom to which Surrealists are convinced a true painter must dedicate himself goes well beyond the social sphere, after all, just as it embraces more than political considerations. This is why they assign Gorky a place of prominence among the artists of our time. They agree with Breton in regarding Gorky's art as "proof that only an absolute purity of means, at the service of unfailing freshness of impression and of a limitless gift for effusion can make possible a leap out of the rut of the known and, with an impeccable arrow of light, point in the present-day direction of liberty."[15]

When speaking of effusion, Breton had something radically different in mind from Rubin. For Breton – and this is essential to our understanding of his outlook as a Surrealist and his perspective on pictorial art – it was the bursting forth of feeling that gave value to Gorky's mature work. André Breton saw that work as proof that the key had turned in the lock which, by 1945, no longer held Arshile Gorky's mind imprisoned in reality, from which it had been set free to roam in surreality.

Notes

1. William S. Rubin, *Dada, Surrealism, and Their Heritage* (New York: The Museum of Modern Art, 1968), 171. The statement is paraphrased in Rubin's *Dada and Surrealist Art* (New York: Abrams, n.d.,), 393.

2. José Pierre, review of the translation of Rubin's *Dada and Surrealist Art*, under the title "Dada, le surréalisme et le ketchup," *La Quinzaine littéraire*, September 16–30, 1975, 16–17. It should be noted in fairness that Rubin is not alone among American art critics in viewing Gorky as he does. Indeed, his discussion of Gorky's role with respect to Surrealism evidences far more caution than one finds among some other commentators.

3. Rubin, *Dada and Surrealist Art*, 123.

4. Harold Rosenberg, *Arshile Gorky: The Man, the Times, the Idea* (New York: Grove Press, 1962), 16.

5. Edward B. Henning, *The Spirit of Surrealism* (Cleveland: The Cleveland Museum of Art, 1979), 140.

6. André Breton, *Le Surréalisme et la peinture,* (Paris: Gallimard, 1965), 199. This definitive edition assembles essays on Surrealism and painting written by Breton between 1925 and 1965.

7. The version of Breton's text printed in the catalogue of Gorky's 1945 show at the Julien Levy Gallery in New York is titled "The Eye-Spring: Arshile Gorky."

8. Breton, *Le Surréalisme et la peinture*, 200.

9. Rubin, *Dada and Surrealist Art*, 402.

10. See William C. Seitz, *Arshile Gorky: Paintings, Drawings, Studies* (New York: The Museum of Modern Art, 1962), 29.

11. Breton, *Le Surréalisme et la peinture*, 200.

12. Rubin, *Dada and Surrealist Art*, 402.

13. Breton, *Le Surréalisme et la peinture*, 200. Except as noted (n. 15, below), all subsequent quotations from Breton are taken from this page.

14. The text appears as the final essay in Breton's *La Clé des champs* (Paris: Les Editions du Sagittaire, 1953), 280–83.

15. Breton, *Le Surréalisme et la peinture*, 201.

Breton, Portrait and Anti-Portrait: From the Figural to the Spectral

Martine Antle

> The portrait of a loved one should not be only an image at which one smiles but also an oracle one questions.
> — Breton

The portrait and the self-portrait engaged Surrealists in all forms of artistic expression: painting, photography, collage, and intaglio. In fact, no other artistic and literary movement has put so much emphasis on the portrait as a medium. The constant need to define, self-define, or displace the representational focus itself is at the center of surrealist ethic, and it holds a place of particular interest for the portrait and the self-portrait. Surrealist portraiture plays on several levels of representation, and the replicated object is often situated *"hors du réel."*[1] The objects lose their iconic function and are inscribed at the limit of the visible and the invisible.

This status of the object is not, however, characteristic of the surrealist representational process. In fact, the theoretical questions raised by surrealist portraiture at large can be associated with Michel Foucault's analysis of *Las Meninas:* "He [the painter] is staring at a point to which, even though it is invisible, we, the spectators, can easily assign an object, since it is we, ourselves, who are that point: our bodies, our faces, our eyes. The spectacle he is observing is doubly invisible."[2] However, Surrealism could not be limited to staging the representational interplay between the "emission point" and the "reception point." Surrealism established some new relationships between the visible and the legible. This new phenomenon, of course best illustrated by Breton's *poème-objet,* establishes a new practice in which "to see" and "to read" are perceived simultaneously. The linguistic sign and the iconic sign can no longer be isolated, and it is from this perspective that Breton's portraits are here viewed, his own self-portraits as well as those by other artists. All of them not only reflect the central role he played in the development of surrealist art but also place him within the collaborative effort dominant in Surrealism. Since Breton approached art criticism selectively rather than chronologically, it seems irrelevant to place these photographs within an historical context. By the same token, even though portraiture as a genre usually raises the question of resemblance and identity, we need only recall how he rejected the traditional opposition between "perception" and "representation"[3] in order to preserve what he called the eye in "a savage state." The artistic pleasure for Breton came from that which is "unnamed" and vanishing: "There is nothing I love so much as that which stretches away before me and *out of sight*. Within the frame of that *unnamed figure, land- or seascape,* I can enjoy an enormous spectacle."[4]

Breton's writings on photography express the same fascination for mystery. He writes on Man Ray:

Il [Man Ray] a choisi bien souvent pour s'exprimer cet instrument moderne, et j'oserai dire, révélateur par excellence: le papier sensible. Le mystère de l'épreuve photographique est intact en ce sens que l'interprétation artistique y est réduite au minimum.[5]

The work of art here places the artist in a position similar to that of the spectator: they both participate in the creative process. Renée Riese Hubert, in her recent book *Surrealism and the Book,* has documented how for Breton "photography should be highly subjective, strictly immediate or instantaneous, a style not normally associated with documentation."[6] The photographs inserted in *Nadja* appear as "a distorting echo," fostering *"hasard objectif* at the expense of mimesis."[7] Semiological studies in art also followed the same vein. Jan Mukarovsky, who was actively involved with the Surrealists in Prague, stressed how

a work of art is not identifiable as psychological aesthetics would like to think it is, with the state of mind and spirit of its creator or with any of the states of mind and spirit induced by its perceivers. Clearly, every state of subjective consciousness involves something individual and momentary that makes it impossible to grasp and communicate in its entirety, whereas the work of art is meant expressly to serve as an intermediary between its creator and the community.[8]

These remarks are the more relevant in the context of Breton's vision of art and the role of the "objective laws of chance" involved in the creative process. The function of Breton's portraits becomes twofold. On the one hand, they are autonomous and call for the participation of the viewer, like any other surrealist work of art. On the other hand, they have a communicative function. Breton, the most important figure in Surrealism, becomes the mediator for Surrealism as well as for his own "oeuvre." These portraits capture a facet of Breton which cannot be found in creative or critical writing. The substance of his philosophy and of his understanding of the arts is caught within the configuration of the portraits and is conveyed through visual means of representation. Therefore, these portraits give us a new perspective into the inner quality which manifests itself in Breton's writing.

The communicative function of Breton's portraits evolves from the objects, their assemblage or their *mise en scène.* Those who photographed him seem to have caught the unusual proximity of the visible and the invisible in his way of looking at things. Just as in *Nadja*, Breton's portraîts relentlessly displace the "who I am" toward the "whom I haunt," the visible toward the invisible, the "figural" toward the "spectral" elements.[9] This infinite search for artistic truth and the "fusion" between the visible and the invisible is present in his poem "Always for the First Time":

Always for the first time
I hardly recognize you by sight
Sometime during the night you come home to a building at an oblique angle
    from my
window
An entirely imaginary structure
. . . .
The definite *fusion* of your *presence* and your *absence*
I've found the secret
Of loving you
For the first time forever.[10]

The portrait becomes a stage strangely animated by objects and their playful shadows. The aesthetic use of detail, in which the image vacillates between the visible and the invisible (the "presence" and the "absence"), the legible and the illegible, is particular to surrealist texts, whether they be pictorial, graphic, photographic, or cinematographic. This use of detail is expressed through the emphasis placed on the medium used for re-presentation and on the spectral motif, both of which elicit recognition of forms blurred by shadows and the accentuated or understated contours of the image.

The figurative portrait or self-portrait (individual or group) in Surrealism denatures the function of figurative portraiture even though the artist is placed directly at the compositional core. The shadowy contrasts, both rendering and obliterating forms, adhere to the same principles governing nonfigurative art.[11] This deflection of the figurative process by means of various techniques, such as photomontage and solarization, undermines the false claim photography has on representation as "certificate of presence."[12] Although Surrealists resorted to using traditional modes of representation, the spectator ceases to travel through real space. Instead, the eye of the spectator is directed toward detail and away from the ensemble, allowing the perspective field to escape observation. The eye wanders from areas of shadow to light, areas of gray to matte or glossy surface, discovering the interior of the visual field itself turned inside out. This visual process stands for artistic creation; the portrait composes its own text using light and contrast.

Writing according to surrealist aesthetics no longer places an image or word in the text; rather it composes the text by traversing incessantly from one mode of representation to another, or from one genre to another. The following discussion of a photograph of the Surrealists, in which Breton is situated at the center, does not actually focus on the group itself, but focuses on an object staged outside the visual field, absent yet always present: the typewriter. Automatic writing is represented here by photographic and pictorial media that serve as signals.

The Effacement of the Authors: *The Surrealist Group in 1924*

The anonymous and untitled portrait *The Surrealist Group in 1924* (Fig. 1) reflects an acute awareness on the part of the photographer of the collective automatic writing process advocated by Breton. This portrait sets the stage for collective automatic writing, reminding us that Breton, however central his role might have been to the surrealist movement, was simply a participant. The progression toward intense darkness at the center of the photograph makes the hands of Simone Breton appear as though they are detached from her body and disengaged from the touch of the typewriter's keyboard. This female personage is set here as a pretext for artistic creation. The spectator's focus of attention is drawn away

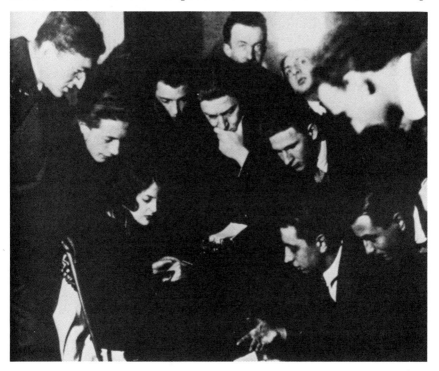

Fig. 1 *The Surrealist Group in 1924.* Left to right: Morise, Vitrac, Boiffard, Breton, Éluard, Naville, de Chirico, Soupault. Bottom: Desnos, Baron; at the typewriter: Simone Breton Collinet.

from the portrait and lured to an object situated in the center of the image, but then it plummets into the darkness of an object barely visible: the typewriter. Finally, the spectator's attention is drawn to the hand of one of the participants. This photograph is in fact centered on the act of writing (the hand) and the act of transcribing (the typewriter). It becomes a representational trap, since it portrays neither the surrealist group as such nor any distinct forms. Only the heads and the hands of the personages emerge from the darkness. Here, the spectral universe is emphasized through the use of shadows and dismembered personages. Even if two figures (from the right and the left) seem to come to the foreground, they appear both visible and invisible simultaneously. It is in the absence of bodies and subject that the automatic text is written. In other words, we participate in the art of writing that is literally photo-graphy – the image writing its own text with circuitous contrastings of light and dark.

Breton's photomontage entitled *L'Écriture automatique* (Fig. 2) shows him in the center of the image. His face and body express *Nadja's* "medical neuter" style: that of an automaton. Behind Breton there is a woman who smiles, and her generic smile provokes us to question the artificial quality of representation. This woman stands behind bars, her hands holding onto the bars in such a way that the bars seem to frame Breton. Here we have a photograph within a photograph: Breton as a veritable automaton. The portrait framed in a photograph moves from subject status to that of object.

The presence of the microscope within the composition serves as a vehicle for exploration, that is to say, for one of the most fundamental goals of Surrealism, according to Breton. Even though Breton has a microscope, he is not looking at what is coming out of it. The enigmatic creatures emerging from the microscope bring out the aesthetic of detail in a manner similar to the preface of *Les Mariés de la tour Eiffel,* in which Cocteau invites us to read his play like a droplet of poetry under a microscope. The microscope, a source of detail, movement, and vanishing representation, participates in the de-composition of the portrait and the image as an ensemble. Everything happens as if the scene were void of figures. As figures/automatons, the personages become in turn the medium for automatic writing. The automatic language and the artificial bodies lead the eye of the spectator of *L'Écriture automatique* to the microscope, the medium of automatic writing. But Breton does not write the text of *L'Écriture automatique* any more than the smiling woman behind bars does: rather, they mime it.

The photomontage and its subtitle are presented as a motif and pretext for the portrait, setting the stage for automatic writing. The text of the photomontage freely moves from the legible (the title) to the visible (the figures/automatons): the scene of *L'Écriture automatique* taking place outside the perceptive field of Breton's portrait. As Barthes would say,

Fig. 2 André Breton, *L'Écriture automatique*, 1938.
Collage. Vera and Arturo Schwarz Collection,
Milan.

"Depth is born at the moment the spectacle itself slowly turns its shadow
toward man and begins to look at him."[13]

Autoportrait: Breton's Mask

Breton did not produce many artistic pieces. He made several collages
such as *"Tragic" à la manière des "comics," Portrait de Gérard,* and *Le Hasard
objectif.* He also collaborated on several "Cadavres exquis." His *Autoportrait* (Fig. 3), presently kept at the Bibliothèque Nationale, might be the
best example of his artistic abilities.

The preceding photomontage by Breton embodies the goals of Surrealism. This linocut is above all a pure reflection of Breton himself. The thea-
tricality of this linocut, and more specifically the use of the mask, is, as I
will show, an objectification of Breton's interiority and his philosophy of
the arts.

At first glance the *Autoportrait* of Breton's face seems to be the motif of
the design and seems to take its graphic point of departure from the

51

Fig. 3   André Breton, *Autoportrait.* Linocut. Bibliothèque Nationale, Paris.

shaded areas delineating the physiognomy. However, the face rapidly
progresses from being figurative to nonfigurative as a result of the strong
contrast in the linocut. The background's fluted texture heightens the
dark intensity of the ink, softening the contours of Breton's face. The
effect is further accentuated by the depiction of the strands of hair. Their
line quality is similar to that of the background texture, modifying the
crown of the head and fragmenting its outline. This depiction of the
strands of hair marks the materialization of the image. Now the image is
better understood in the context of tactility and movement, augmenting
the uncompleted and fragmentary aspect of pictorial representation. The
referent in the image is lost in the detail, and the receding ensemble of the
perceptive field sends us back to the image's modes of representation
again and again.

   Thus the modes of representation in portraiture cross over into the theatrical. The face decomposes, taking on the aspects of a universal mask.
This theatrical mask signals the death of the personage while "empêchant
tout excés dans l'expressivité comme toute référence trop précise à un
individu-corps."[14] Breton becomes the specter and the artifact of
representation.

The crossing of portraiture and theatre appears again in another portrait of Breton, taken by Man Ray in 1930, in which the mask prevails (Fig. 4). Here Breton wears a pair of aviator goggles and his face is framed in a white rectangle that adds to the inexpressiveness of the figure. It is precisely this displacement of the photograph toward theatre that, according to Barthes, makes photography an art and a form of revelation: "Rien ne distingue, eidétiquement [. . .] une photographie d'une peinture [. . .]. Ce n'est pourtant pas [. . .] par la peinture que la photographie touche à l'art, c'est par le théâtre."[15] Given a mask, the face makes the photograph into a type of "théâtre primitif [. . .] figuration de la face immobile [. . .] sous laquelle nous voyons les morts."[16] Thus, the spectral characteristic of the personage is accentuated by a mask which leaves the origin of speech (the mouth) free to emit nothing but a masked voice, taking its point of origin not within the photograph, but outside, toward the theatrical.

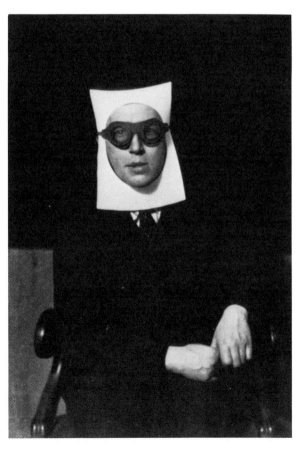

Fig. 4   Man Ray, *André Breton,* c. 1930. Collection Lucien Treillard, Paris.

53

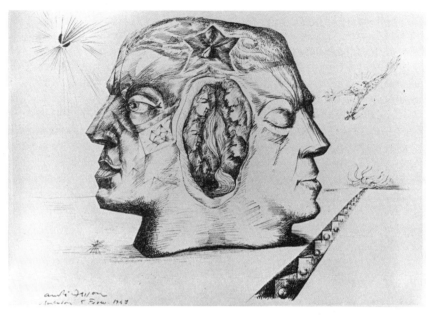

Fig. 5   André Masson, *Portrait d'André Breton,* 1941. Galerie Louise Leiris, Paris.

Breton and His Double

The *Portrait d'André Breton,* a pen and India ink drawing executed by André Masson in 1941 (Fig. 5), presents two faces of Breton: one fixed (eyes closed) and the other (eyes open) with its facial contours inscribed in ink, suggesting movement within the representation. The joining of these two faces into one invites the spectator to find a signification, but, once again, the image says nothing to us. The portrait ultimately becomes lost in a void ("un non-lieu") which is that of the steps sketched obliquely at the base of the drawing, tracing what rises only to be lost to infinity and the vanishing point of representation.[17] The void created by the fleeting image unites the *Portrait d'André Breton* (the visual) with the poem *Fata Morgana* (the text) written by Breton: "C'est la pièce sans entr'actes le rideau levé une fois pour toutes sur la cascade."[18] The inner and outer representation of Breton presented by the two joined faces now becomes a mirror of the title *Fata Morgana* and its meaning, which is extended both to a mythic dimension as well as to a physical phenomenon:

Fata Morgana is more than an invocation of a pagan goddess. . . . *It is a mirage* produced by the refraction of the dawn's light on the Calabrese Coast and in the delta of Messina on mornings when the sea is still and the sun rises over the mountains and strikes the Mediterranean *at a forty-five-degree angle.* It creates phantasmagoria. . . .[19]

54

The mirage effect Balakian perceived and explained in the poem of this period is also recognizable in Masson's portrait of Breton. It helps us to understand better the joining of the two faces and the simulated movement from-or-to a forty-five-degree angle. We can also speculate that the diamond which reveals the contours of a starfish could be the medium of "refraction."

At the center of the portrait of the two faces joined together appears an orifice where the female faces of the poem loom up before us: "Têtes de femmes qui se succèdent sur tes épaules quand tu dors."[20] This aperture in the portrait sets the stage for eroticism, which Breton has described as a "cérémonie fastueuse dans un souterrain." Artifact or convergence of multiple faces once loved leading to nowhere, such is the theatre of mad-love: "La scène . . . est barrée . . . ce sont les femmes qu'il a aimées, qui l'ont aimé, celles-ci des années, celles-là un jour. Comme il fait noir."[21] The portrait here is shielded from representation by the endless game of signs circulating, from pictorial to poetic toward the theatrical. What is represented here is the work of art "sur toutes ses faces extérieures, intérieures."[22]

Breton: A Prop in a Showcase?

The collage-box entitled *André Breton* and executed by Joseph Cornell (Fig. 6) puts Breton on stage as well as in a box (*"mis en boîte"*). Around the portrait of Breton (taken by Man Ray), there is an array of objects that principally suggest travel, but to nowhere in particular. Objects like an obliterated postmarked stamp from which one can recognize the destination, but not the point of departure, or the night bird of prey, the owl,[23] act to decentralize the space that Breton's figure occupies. Cornell's choice of objects presents the activities of Breton: his travels as well as the exploration of the subconscious. Moreover, these objects assume a certain mobility within the box which enables them to be displaced easily as in a theatrical set, and permits the work of art to be re-composed "ad infinitum." Breton is made to serve as a theatrical prop.

If at first glance the photograph of Breton in the collage attracts the focus of attention, it is quickly pushed to the background as representational decor. Breton's solarized portrait creates an effect of photographic relief and assumes a spectral aspect through its contrasting tones of gray and through the halo around the head. Using solarization, the portrait functions rather like an anti-portrait, since the medium emphasizes the process of creating the image rather than the image itself. We recall that the same process was used in another of Man Ray's photographs, entitled *Imprint of Matter on Thought (Primat de la matière sur la pensée)*. The collage allies itself with solarization in order to present us with a scene behind the pseudo-figurative motif. It is a scene void of real personage, yet the ob-

Fig. 6   Joseph Cornell, *André Breton,* c. 1960. Collage-box. 17¾ × 14¾ × 1⅜ in. Estate of Joseph Cornell.

jects of artistic creation come to the forefront and present the spectator with a moment in which the work of art unceasingly does and undoes itself.

56

This Is NOT a Portrait

The portraits of Breton, whether they were intended as figurative or nonfigurative, cease to function as a depiction of Breton himself. They constantly bring forth the question of the subject as specter of itself. Breton is foremost an element or pre-text of representation: mime, automaton, mask, or double; a fictitious figure, always uncompleted, who beckons the game, the laceration in the linocut. The portraits always invite the spectator to participate, to do and undo representation.

These portraits uniquely present Breton-as-object of representation, while staging the fundamental basis for his philosophy of Surrealism, whether it be the exploration of the subconscious, travelling, or the poetic experience. It is within the visual that the person and the "oeuvre" meet. At the same time, these portraits place Surrealism in the sphere of the legible and the visible, which sends us once again to the message of Breton's *poème-objet*.

As representational objects, it is not enough that the portraits of Breton simply bring into consideration the central place he holds in Surrealism. They capture the spectator's eye with modes of re-presentation in which the image circulates. In surrealist portraiture, both photography and painting, the pictorial, the poetic, and the theatrical worlds unite to present an exceedingly subtle moment in which the work of art, fleeting and spectral, inscribes itself between signs.

Notes

1. Hans Bellmer, *Petite anatomie de l'inconscient physique ou anatomie de l'image* (Paris: Le Terrain Vague, 1957), unpag.

2. Michel Foucault, "Las Meninas," in *Calligram. Essays in New Art History from France,* ed. Norman Bryson (Cambridge: Cambridge University Press, 1988), 92.

3. "All the experimentation in progress would be of a nature to demonstrate that perception and representation, which seem to the ordinary adult to be opposed one to the other in such a radical manner, should be deemed only the products of dissociation of a single, initial faculty, whose eidic image finds response and of which traces are found in the primitive and the child." André Breton, *Point du jour,* 250, cited in Anna Balakian, *André Breton* (New York: Oxford University Press, 1971), 153.

4. André Breton, *Surrealism and Painting,* in Herschel B. Chipp, *Theories of Modern Art. A Source Book by Artists and Critics.* (Berkeley: University of California Press, 1968), 404.

5. André Breton, *Oeuvres complètes,* vol. 1 (Paris: Gallimard, 1988), 299.

6. Renée Riese Hubert, *Surrealism and the Book* (Berkeley: University of California Press, 1988), 258.

7. Ibid., 259.

8. Jan Mukarovsky, "Art as a Semiotic Fact," in *Semiotics of Art,* ed. Ladislav Metjka and Irwin R. Titunik (Cambridge: Massachusetts Institute of Technology, 1986), 3.

9. On several occasions Breton expresses his fascination for the "spectral" character of representation. See, for example, his "Introduction to the World of Toyen," in *Toyen* (Paris: Éditions Sokolova, 1953), 77.

10. André Breton, "Always for the First Time," in Michael Benedikt, *The Poetry of Surrealism. An Anthology* (Boston: Little, Brown, 1974), 126–27, my emphasis.

11. René Passeron distinguishes nonfigurative art from abstract art: "La non-figuration n'est pas toujours l'aboutissement d'un mouvement ascétique vers une pureté impliquant la disparition des formes ressemblantes." Passeron, *L'Oeuvre picturale et les fonctions de l'apparence* (Paris: Librairie Philosophique J. Vrin, 1986), 279.

12. According to Barthes the photographic portrait abolishes any notion of temporality; it reflects nothing more than the image of a fragmentary and lost moment, leading the subject to the following: "Je ne suis ni un sujet ni un objet mais plutôt un sujet qui se sent devenir objet: je vis alors une micro-expérience de la mort (de la parenthèse). Je deviens vraiment spectre." Roland Barthes, *La Chambre claire. Note sur la photographie* (Paris: Gallimard/Le Seuil, 1980), 30.

13. Barthes, 115.

14. Anne Ubersfeld, *L'École du spectateur. Lire le théâtre 2* (Paris: Les Editions Sociales, 1981), 231.

15. Barthes, 55.

16. Ibid, 56.

17. It is precisely beyond the steps that surrealist humor explodes in *L'Anthologie de l'humour noir:* "La porte de la pièce étant ouverte, on découvrait à travers celle du vestibule l'espace qui *s'étendait au delà du palier et les premières marches de l'escalier.*" (Breton, *L'Anthologie de l'humour noir* [Paris: Jean-Jacques Pauvert, 1966], 454, my emphasis). "Il vous est arrivé de mettre le pied, dans le noir, *sur la dernière marche de l'escalier, celle qui n'existe pas?* (547, my emphasis).

18. André Breton, *Fata Morgana,* in *Poèmes* (Paris: Gallimard, 1948), 185.

19. Balakian, 185, my emphasis.

20. Breton, *Fata Morgana,* 189.

21. André Breton, *L'Amour fou* (Paris: Gallimard, 1937), 8.

22. Ibid., 17.

23. It is ironic that the owl by definition is "a night bird of prey found throughout the world" with "a soft plumage which permits noiseless flight: applied figuratively to a person of nocturnal habits, solemn appearance." *Webster's New World Dictionary of the American Language* (New York: World Publishing, 1970), 1015.

The Surrealist Libido: André Breton's *"Poisson soluble,* No. 8"

Michael Riffaterre

There exists an essential relationship between desire and language, and even more so between desire and the representation of reality in literature. Desire implies the absence or inaccessibility of its object. Similarly, the object referred to by a word is not usually itself present. The constitutive elements of signs, linguistic or not, bear this out: signifier, signified, and referent. Whether or not the referent is present, the signifier in any case presupposes the absence of the signified.

The subject of this article is this analogy between desire and writing, and the role played by the representation of desire in the production of the text. Surrealism, with its great interest in the erotic, in both its conscious and unconscious forms, and in particular the author of a book called *L'Amour fou* [*Mad Love*], would seem to offer an especially rich source for such an enquiry. The aforementioned presupposition of absence can also refer to the case of desire generated by the lack of a signified. This presuppositional libido finds itself transferred to signifieds derived from the initial verbal given. These signifieds are words or groups of words that correspond to components of the semantic structure of that given: they emphatically repeat fragments, synecdoches of the first referent. The initial lack of object is thus recalled, exacerbating our need to recover it.

Starting with these rather abstract premises, I would like to propose the rules of transformation that govern the generation of the literary text, which consists in changing the first word designating an object of desire into a series of phrases or sentences. An object can be defined as desirable according to categories that are already established and stereotyped in language: *money, woman,* and *power* are words at the top of the male ladder of desirability. These paradigms contain variants whose only function is to designate that desirability: *daughter of Eve,* in the Romantic era, or *a Venus,* or *a nymph* in the eighteenth-century texts, or, in naturalistic texts that purport to reproduce colloquial language, metonyms like *skirt.* Syntax itself also represents desire: a verb expressing desire is enough to make its direct object desirable; an admiring adjective is all that is necessary to make the noun thus modified admirable. Grammar seems to employ the ninth proposition of Spinoza's *Ethics:* "We neither seek nor desire an object because we believe it to be good; on the contrary, we judge it to be good because we desire it." The description of desire thus consists in projecting onto an object the libido of the perceiving subject.

Just as hope, once fulfilled, ceases to be hope, desire can only be represented in terms of a frustrated present, or of a future, in the anticipation of what is to come. Desire is to description what suspense is to narrative. Lasting only as long as it remains unsatisfied, desire can only be depicted through suspense or through delay. Its literary representations cannot be confused with the mimesis of possession, as would be the case in a recounting of sexual fantasy.

Any representation of desire contains an element of desirability (hope, for example) and an element of interdiction. The latter prevents the former from attaining its goal. I would like to propose a rule of saturation and a rule of displacement. Saturation occurs when all nouns in the text receive a positive or negative marker, according to whether anticipation or frustration is being emphasized. Displacement occurs when the nouns in the text are metonyms of the desired object, the representation of which is thus displaced onto an inaccessible place or moment. The more metonyms there are, the more the representation emphasizes the fact that it remains incomplete, and that the desired object remains hidden, at least in its totality.

If the rules of saturation and metonymic displacement are valid, they should be especially applicable to texts written "under the dictation of the subconscious." This is the phrase by which André Breton, in the *Manifeste du surréalisme* (1924), defined the new mode of poetic inspiration that was to put an end to the traditional literature characterized by labored style, repeated corrections, emphasis on the approximation of manner to matter, the pursuit of the *mot juste* – what the Surrealists called the *littérature de calcul* ("literature of calculation"). In the latter they saw arbitrary conventions, artifice, the tired and tiring repetition of all-too-familiar themes. Breton intended to replace all this with what he called "automatic writing." Critics have long refused to believe it an authentic product of the unconscious. It was to resemble the recorded product of the "evenly hovering attention" which is the counterpart in psychoanalysis to free association, but the Surrealists were suspected of systematizing it according to the models furnished by Freud, and similar accusations were leveled at their accounts of dreams. Nonetheless, if automatic writing is not an immediate product of the unconscious, it does attempt to represent it, and such an effort can only result in writing that conforms to verbal association, in all its arbitrariness. And yet this very arbitrariness is obsessive, already informed by cliché. The authenticity of such an endeavor, which is undoubtedly adulterated on a psychological level, regains its purity in linguistic terms. The rules that I have proposed will therefore obtain, as my example will demonstrate.

Sur la montagne Sainte-Geneviève il existe un large abreuvoir où viennent se rafraîchir à la nuit tombée tout ce que Paris compte encore de bêtes troublantes, de plantes à surprises. Vous le croiriez desséché si, en examinant les choses de plus près, vous ne voyiez glisser capricieusement sur la pierre un petit filet rouge que rien ne peut tarir. Quel sang précieux continue donc à couler en cet endroit que les plumes, les duvets, les poils blancs, les feuilles déchlorophyllées qu'il longe détournent de son but apparent? Quelle princesse de sang royal se consacre ainsi après sa disparition à l'entretien de ce qu'il y a de plus souverainement tendre dans la faune et la flore de ce pays? Quelle sainte au tablier de roses a fait couler cet extrait divin dans les veines de la pierre? Chaque soir le merveilleux moulage plus beau qu'un sein s'ouvre à des levres nouvelles et la vertu désaltérante du sang de rose se communique à tout le ciel environnant, pendant que sur une borne grelotte un jeune enfant qui compte les étoiles; tout à l'heure il reconduira son troupeau aux crins millénaires, depuis le sagittaire ou flèche d'eau qui a trois mains, l'une pour extraire, l'autre pour caresser, l'autre pour ombrager ou pour diriger, depuis le sagittaire de mes jours jusqu'au chien d'Alsace qui a un oeil bleu et un oeil jaune, le chien des anaglyphes de mes rêves, le fidèle compagnon des marées.

(*Poisson soluble*, No. 8)

(On Sainte Geneviève Hill there is a broad watering-trough where, at nightfall, what Paris still has of disturbing beasts, of surprising plants, come to refresh themselves. You would think it had run dry if, on closer inspection, you didn't see sliding capriciously over the stone a small red trickle that nothing can dry up. What precious blood, then, still flows in this place, that the feathers, the down, the white hairs, the dechlorophyllated leaves which it passes divert from its apparent course? What royal-blooded princess devotes herself after she's gone to the upkeep of all that is most sovereignly tender in the flora and fauna of this country? What saint with apron of roses has made this divine essence flow in the veins of the rock? Each evening the wonderful hollow cast, more beautiful than a breast, opens itself to new lips, and the thirst-quenching power of the rose-blood spreads to all the surrounding sky, while on a boundary-stone shivers a young child who counts the stars; soon he will drive home his herd with their millennial hides, from the sagittaria or arrowhead that has three hands, one for distilling essences, the other for caressing, the other for casting shadows or for leading, from the sagittaria of my days to the Alsatian dog with one blue eye and one yellow eye, dog of the anaglyphs of my dreams, faithful companion of the tides.)

[*Soluble Fish*, No. 8, trans. Elisabeth Ladenson]

The text in question is a prose-poem which seems to approach verbal delirium. It is by André Breton, from a collection entitled *Poisson soluble* [*Soluble Fish*]. This title, which appears at first to be nothing more than a joke, in fact symbolizes the automatism of the unconscious, since it suggests that its author has disappeared, dissolved. The image is as appropriate as it is bizarre, since it applies to the zodiac-minded Breton, born under the sign of Pisces.

The poem does not, at first glance, even seem to represent desire. It sketches a nocturnal scene, a landscape paradoxically uniting city and country. In the very center of Paris, in the heart of the Latin Quarter, on the *montagne Sainte-Geneviève*, flows a miraculous spring, the watering-hole where fantastic animals slake their thirst. Near this spring, a young shepherd watches over a herd that is just as strange, since instead of sheep, the creatures of the zodiac graze under his care. The spring itself is a supernatural phenomenon because blood flows from it in place of water, the blood from the sacrifice of a young princess.

The reader will easily recognize in this the well-known legend of the miraculous spring whose pure water flows at the scene of a crime, where a virgin shepherdess has been raped and murdered; the crystal clarity of the flowing water either effaces the traces of wrongdoing, or else symbolizes the victim's purity. A recent version of this legend can be found in Ingmar Bergman's film *Virgin Spring,* in which the shepherdess is made into a princess, as in the Breton poem, in fact, although in the latter the only reference to the victim's identity is made in the form of questions.

The bloody spring in the poem is, certainly, different from the usual version of the legend, but a series of images announces that this blood has the mysterious property of quenching thirst, which confirms that its mythic function is identical to that of water, and that this blood is a desirable liquid.

From "precious blood" (*sang précieux*) to the "rose-blood" (*sang de rose*) that spreads its thirst-quenching power in the sky, the successive images are all variants of the magic potion motif. Its praise is repeated, directly or indirectly, in synonymic forms, although some are to be taken literally, others figuratively. The expression "royal blood," for example, can literally designate the blood of a monarch, or it can simply be a metonym for "royal princess" (*princesse de sang*). "Essence" (*extrait*) is a word borrowed from the vocabulary of chemistry, and specifically that of perfume-making; it refers to the precious liquid distilled from rose petals that is used in the rarest perfumes. The poetic equivalent of this essence is in fact in French *sang des roses* ("blood of roses," or "rose-blood"). "Precious blood" literally signifies exactly that, but it's also, in religious discourse, the commonplace term for the blood of Christ (*sang précieux*). As for the blood that spreads through the sky, it recalls another myth, an intertext that lends meaning to our text: the image alludes to the myth of Juno forced to suckle Hercules at her breast, despite the child's being Jupiter's bastard. Caught in her sleep, she turns and pushes the infant's mouth away from the breast that he has already grasped. But the divine infant's suction is so powerful that the stream of milk still flowing from the nipple spreads across the night sky: thus was the Milky Way created.

And so the "wonderful hollow cast, more beautiful than a breast" that nightly "opens itself to new lips" has a mythological intertext that links the rosy blood of the poem with the original thirst-quencher, milk, but it also in itself could hardly be more obviously an object of erotic desire. The image of the cast of a breast both belongs to an erotic tradition and contains a surrealist reversal of the familiar hyperbolic comparison of a woman's beauty to that of a statue. This hollow mold surpasses a real breast in beauty: it is the cliché that can be found in such works as Bulwer-Lytton's *Last Days of Pompeii:* the shapely woman perishes in the catastrophe, but her beauty is preserved in imprint form in the lava.

The blood that then flows across the sky is, by virtue of its galactic intertext and its stated thirst-quenching powers, endowed with desirability. It is through the persistence of such positive connotations, in spite of the diversity of the representations that they affect, and in spite of the inconsistencies and contradictions of the mimesis, that we recognize the textual saturation that makes the desired object desirable. Nonsense at the semantic level in no way threatens significance at the semiotic level.

But the question remains: why is this blood made into an object of desire? Is it a matter of rape fantasies? These are frequent in literature in which a shepherdess, alone and defenseless in the countryside, symbolizes feminine vulnerability, in the same way as does Little Red Riding Hood trotting toward the waiting jaws of the Big Bad Wolf. Stendhal, in his treatise *On Love,* chose the shepherdess seduced in the solitude of woods and prairies as an extreme example of the brief fling, to emphasize by contrast the slowness with which real passion grows. In any case, shepherdesses have been conventional objects of desire in literature since the first rustic idylls; in the bucolic genre, they represent sexuality.

These rape fantasies are, however, edulcorated, purged of their violence, and the victim, encouraged by the complicity of Nature, rapidly consents, and does not get murdered. Even if she is murdered, like the mythical princess, or devoured, like Little Red Riding Hood (with hunger standing in for another appetite), the blood that she sheds is a consequence of the act, and not itself an object of desire. Far from being used in place of water to wash out the crime, that blood defiles.

Here, not only is the blood sacralized and desirable, it also represents the shepherdess herself. The key to this transference is provided by the end of the poem, in which the shepherd-dog appears: "Alsatian dog with one blue eye and one yellow eye, dog of the anaglyphs of my dreams, faithful companion of the tides." The word "anaglyph," with its archaeological ring, refers to the blue eye and yellow eye of the dog: an anaglyph is a kind of old-fashioned stereoscope, a gadget or toy that used superimposed complementary colors to create an effect of relief (like 3-D glasses in the movies of the fifties). In the "magic lantern" tradition, the anaglyph is another positive marker, connecting the dog to the satisfaction of desire, in dream and magic projection. The dog itself is represented less as the guardian of the herd than in terms of the cliché of canine loyalty: he is the "faithful companion of the shepherd" or "of the shepherdess." But the word "shepherdess" is, bizarrely, repressed, and replaced by the tide, by the ebb and flow of the sea: "faithful companion of the tides." The plural is important. Implication always expresses what it hides, hence the inevitable conclusion, especially given this context of blood, that "tides," suppressing the designation of a woman, must be read as a metaphor for menstruation.

As soon as the reader makes this discovery, the nonsense disappears. The text could conceivably have been interpreted as the mimesis of a dream, but here the paradox of an urban setting imbued with incompatible images of a scene from country life reveals itself as a variant of the structure simultaneously uniting and opposing the desirable and the off-limits. While the blood is described as desirable, it is also prohibited, since menstrual blood is impure blood in all Western religious traditions. As soon as this idea occurs, it actualizes the rule of frustration: after all, the Bible prohibits intercourse with a woman during her period. In consequence, both miraculously thirst-quenching spring and taboo liquid, menstrual blood is a perfect metaphor for desire.

Nevertheless, as a work of art, our prose-poem presents images that appear totally arbitrary; the fusion of two incompatible settings, urban and rustic, remains entirely gratuitous, and its relation to the blood symbolism remains far-fetched. And yet the poetic text is always overdetermined and overmotivated: it must impose itself with all the force of proof, the more so if its form is disconcerting.

To be sure, Saint Geneviève is the patron saint of Paris, and she was both a princess and a shepherdess, but this is not enough to transform Paris into a pasture, and after all, she never spilled her blood, nor lost her honor. But it is precisely at the moment when our perplexity is at its height that a crucial element becomes apparent: the most bizarre, the most seemingly absurd word of the poem, the word whose strangeness is incompatible even with the miraculous-spring motif, furnishes us with the key to these images, destroys their randomness and lends motivation to what had seemed gratuitous. Granted, this word heralds the appearance of a shepherd with his herd, but it does so in the context of Paris, where such an apparition should be unexpected, and it spoils, in a way, the legendary atmosphere created by an enchanted spring. It's this double strangeness that makes it stand out, because it bothers us as long as a revelatory linkage that will finally make this word marvelously appropriate has not been established, appropriate at once to the rustic setting, to the shepherdess, to Paris and to the symbolism of desire that these three elements are hiding. The very diversity reveals it, now that it has become apparent, as a triple appropriateness.

This key word is *abreuvoir* (watering-trough). The miraculous spring does not flow from within the earth, as we would expect even in the literature of the fantastic, it flows from a watering-trough. This word *abreuvoir*, which is found only in the vocabulary of animal husbandry, and would seem appropriate only in a realistic description of a farm, is actually closely related to an exclusively poetic term, one used only in very conventional literary contexts, the verb *abreuver* or *s'abreuver*, "to slake thirst." Moreover, the thirst in question is metaphorical thirst (it is more rarely used in a literal sense, but in that case it is always melodramatic), the thirst for blood, as in *s'abreuver du sang de l'ennemi,* "to slake one's thirst for enemy blood," certainly a desirable activity.

This bloodthirsty hyperbole would have been long forgotten, buried in the rhetoric of polemic propaganda, traditional satire, or outdated epics, were it not kept alive in the French national anthem. No French reader can go from *abreuvoir* to *s'abreuver* without recognizing this intertext, of which he is reminded at every public event. All French schoolchildren are forced to learn at least one of the verses of the *Marseillaise,* which contains the following lines:

Entendez-vous dans les campagnes
Mugir ces féroces soldats?
Ils viennent jusque dans nos bras
Egorger nos fils, nos compagnes.
Aux armes, citoyens! Formez vos bataillons!
Marchons, marchons!
Qu'un sang impur abreuve nos sillons!

(Do you hear those ferocious soldiers bellow in the countryside? They're coming right for us to slaughter our sons and our wives. Citizens, take up arms! Form your battalions, let's march, let's march! May our fields [furrows] be slaked with impure blood!)

Impure blood, the thirst for this blood, and the word *sillons* (furrows), rather than *champs* (fields) or *labours* (plowed land), as metonyms for *campagnes* (countryside), as well as the rhyme that associates *sillons* with *compagnes,* that is to say, women – all these elements are now in place to form a series of double meanings that sketch the outline of a woman who satisfies a metaphorical thirst. Now *sang impur* can also refer to menstrual blood, and the word *sillon* is a salacious euphemism for the female genitals; the imperative form of the verb for thirst-slaking expresses a program of desire. *Sillon* in the intertext caps a paradigm of erotically charged images of hollowness: the watering-trough, the cast of a breast, even the anaglyph (which also refers to ornamental carving, and comes from the Greek verb "to hollow out"); the furrow simply provides the most obvious allusion to the female genitals.

In case my argument still does not seem convincing, I would like to add that the *montagne Sainte-Geneviève* on which Breton situates his poetic spring is no ordinary hill. First of all, it is to Paris what the Capitoline Hill is to Rome. But what is relevant for our purposes is that, when Paris was Lutetia, the Latin name of the *montagne Sainte-Geneviève* was *mons Veneris,* the hill dedicated to the goddess of desire. Better still, mons veneris, in old-fashioned medical terminology, designates the part of the female sex just above the clitoris. In the French national anthem, in traditional topography, and in female anatomy, the same words are both a symbol of consecration and an invitation to desecration.

The instinct that so powerfully incites us to go back and forth between the two opposing poles of the sacred is the dynamic manifestation of the complementary relationship between seduction and interdiction, inseparable as two sides of the same coin. It is this polarity, and the equivalence or interchangeability of opposites manifested in a single word, or in words as close to one another as a noun and verb with the same root (abreuvoir/abreuver), that gives rise to texts of this sort, that do not appear to represent desire, nor even to refer to anything recognizable. But the apparent absurdity does not free the reader, who at first glance may think he has escaped the constraints of authorial intention, the traps set by an art whose aim is to manipulate him. Such constraints are in fact replaced by those, infinitely more rigorous and effective, of verbal associations. Far from obtaining only in the linearity of the text, these associations are also made between the lines of the written text and their complements or opposites in the intertext. It is the intertext that gives the reader the means to recover the representation of reality that has been overthrown or censored by the textual non-sense. Once recovered, the representation of the real is sufficiently unusual and unmotivated to serve as a launching pad for the reader's search for the metaphor or metonym of desire that alone accounts for the choice of the object represented.

This reading process, in the course of which interpretation, the discovery of the actual meaning of the literary text or of its real focus of interest, the discovery of what its form, images and story disguise – the discovery, finally, of its symbolism, of the fact that what is said on the surface of the text is only a figure for a significance hidden in the intertext – this whole process is analogous to the listening process in psychoanalysis. The text as read is like the patient's conscious discourse, while the intertext, repressed by the text but recovered by the analyst-reader, is the unconscious for which that discourse serves as a screen. The key, once again, the means of passing from the text to the intertext, the tool of that self-analysis known as reading literature, that is, reading it from the standpoint of its literariness, is a word whose two sides, conscious and unconscious, textual and intertextual, are suddenly detected by the reader, either under the pressure of a difficulty in reading (accounting for a watering-trough in an enigmatic text), or under the pressure of a repetition that appears unjustified, or seems to be a stylistic mistake, an awkward phrasing, or a gratuitous game.

Reading Breton Today:
"La Mort rose"
Ronnie Scharfman

> The mind, that ocean where each kind
> Does straight its own resemblance find;
> Yet it creates, transcending these,
> Far other worlds and other seas,
> Annihilating all that's made
> To a green thought in a green shade.
> Andrew Marvell, "The Garden"

My intention in this essay will be to explore "La Mort rose," a poem from what I'll call Breton's high classic surrealist period, dating from 1932 in the collection *Le Revolver à cheveux blancs,* and to confront it with contemporary critical instruments in order to see how, if indeed, a high classic surrealist text can be read. I do not seek here to give a reading reducible to any totalizing hermeneutic. Rather, with the aid of some critical devices available to us as readers today, I would like to look at the way this text suggests ways of reading it as it unfolds.

We can read André Breton more comprehensively today because we have had at our disposal such seminal texts as Michael Riffaterre's "La Métaphore filée dans la poésie surréaliste," Ricardou's reflections on the "nouveau roman," Kristeva's concept of intertextuality, Saussure's notion of the anagram, Rastier's elaboration of Greimas's isotopes, Benveniste's analyses of "L'Homme dans la langue," and, especially, Xavière Gauthier's revisions of Freudian and Lacanian theory in *Surréalisme et sexualité.*[1]

From the poem's inception, that is, from its title, "La Mort rose," we are faced with a dilemma: how to account for the simultaneous presence of fragile and violent images, of a delicate voice pronouncing irreparable loss? And how do we read an intimate love lyric which is couched in terms of cosmic cataclysm? Is the poem the definition of its title, a semantic equivalent whose reading would consist of, among other things, identifying those semes present in the defined title in nucleus form that are disseminated throughout the text in isotopic networks? If the poem promises a magical mystery tour in its first verse by surreally joining two different phenomenological registers, the marine and the aerial, to form new creatures of easy flight, "pieuvres ailées," it is quick to transform the free-

67

dom so suggested by the temporal qualifications of "une dernière fois" and "la veillé unique," connoting an imminent end and even a last judgment.

This rhythm of rupture and recommencement is paradigmatic for the text, and has a productive, multiplicative function, paradoxically moving the text forward into a future which signifies its own end. The text proceeds by producing series of images, communal lexicons, whose density of interrelations requires that the reader isolate them, only to find that they are, so to speak, inherently contaminated. This problem of an originary fusion of signifying elements structures the poem's affect as well as its generation. To be more precise, let us take the next verse: "Tu sentiras monter dans tes cheveux le soleil blanc et noir." The poet's voice, addressing the "tu" here for the first time, imagines a fusion between the love object and the cosmos, the implicit comparison being between the strands of hair and the rays of light. Superimposed, this already echoes the "pieuvres ailées," and its reiteration establishes an isotope of what I will call sur-membering. But at the same time, the cosmic mingles with the personal as both "blanc et noir," and here the simultaneity of a dual valorization of the same experience opens that gaping breach which is known in affective terms as ambivalence, and in signifying terms as ambiguity. But are these images not already redundant versions of the poem's very title? Moreover, the layering of meaning has only begun. The light isotope is activated here in the first of its actualizations, already containing the double-edged capacity to illuminate or blind. And the image may also invoke the myth of Medusa, whose snake-infested head Perseus cuts off at the risk of his life. The intertextual allusion sets in motion another series of images, which constitute what I shall call a dismembering isotope, whose most frequent actualization may be seen in the form of some male castration-anxiety image.

If every image is so over-determined, where can the reader begin to extricate and dissociate in order to isolate possible readings? Benveniste would tell us that we should look to the "je-tu" relationship in the text. Indeed, there is much to say about the way these two are articulated in this poetic discourse. Benveniste explains that "je" can only constitute itself by positing a "tu," that their relationship is dialectical.[2] Here we have a series of predictions, prophesied by the poetic voice and addressed to the "tu," in which she is the passive spectator or even victim of cosmic and personal transformation resulting in her abandonment, a kind of "pink death": "tu sentiras," "tu observeras," "tu verras." The first intervention of the speaking subject in the text beyond that of the prophetic voice is one of a dismembered allusion to the poet, projecting a kind of future past for the poem, an apparition perhaps capable of regeneration beyond death, but nonetheless cut off from its source: "Sur un pêcher en fleurs apparaîtront les mains qui écrivirent ces vers." The hands are no sooner observed than they, too, undergo metamorphosis, thus entering the world of shifting insubstantiality which is one of the underlying sources of anguish in this poem. This reference to writing, that is, to the poem and to its inevitable transmutation, is a poignant allusion to the tension in the text between the changes it generates as it proceeds, the irresistible fate it both produces and records, and its motivation as writing to salvage itself from the wreck of erasure.

The next intervention of the subject finds it fused with "tu" into "nous" where the cosmos, out of control despite the poet's efforts to predict it all, is "plus fort que nous." The repetition of this locution, "plus fort que," seen earlier in the poem as "liqueur plus forte que la mort," establishes the battle as a life and death one – will death win out over "us," or vice versa? When the poet finally establishes himself in the poem as a true grammatical subject, it is to ask the essential question concerning a linguistic and experiential reciprocity, one that confesses to the difficulty of committing poetic gynocide: "Que ferai-je du tremblement de ta voix?" The poet's efforts thus far to extricate, to dissociate himself from the future he is prophesying for the "tu" will have been in vain, for, to the extent that they are dialectically linked, linguistically and amorously, one cannot disappear without the other. And, in effect, as the litany of what the future holds in store for the "tu" proceeds, it is echoed by a future which the subject cannot avoid for itself: to the enumeration "tu mentiras," "tu te promèneras," "tu t'y égratineras," "tu n'auras pas à tirer," "tu arriveras," corresponds now "que ferai-je," "je monterai," "ma faim tournoiera," "elle nattera les cheveux," "j'appartiendrai au vide," "mes rêves seront formels et vains," "je m'introduirai," "mes appels te laisseront." The demiurgic voice sometimes manages to distance itself from the "je-tu" relationship long enough to make pronouncements whose thrust is more global, more encompassing, less personalized, as if to mitigate the tragedy, to reassure, to lighten the blow, by extricating itself. Yet another relationship is established here, of "us" versus the universe and time, even as all relationships seem to be blown apart, in flux, or regrouping.

If we isolate these announcements, what can they tell us? I see a different quality to the following verses from the ones under discussion until now: "Et tout passera dans l'amour indivisible," "Mais la peur n'existera déjà plus," "Mais les noms des amants seront oubliés." They constitute a micro-poem within the text itself, setting up a signifying chain of their own. The first proclaims total fusion within love; the second, as if by reaction, reassures that this state would be beyond fear, will have transcended and annihilated fear; the last, shedding a more ambiguous light on the previous statements, addresses oblivion as perhaps the price one pays for the reassurance of fusion, a price about which the poem and poet are ambivalent.

All this, yet still the text has not produced a why – what is the event, textual or emotional? Is there a reading under this reading, a different semiotic map which we have not charted yet which motivates the poem and activates its imagistic networks? What of the actual vehicles in the poem itself, instruments of motion? We have seen, in the first verse, the "pieuvres ailées," without specifically noting them as a kind of magical male fantasy of flying phalluses. At the end of the poem, we find the chiasmatic inversion of this image in the "train fait de tortues de glace." Such earth-bound creatures are not only interminably slow, they are actually frozen into immobility, paralyzed yet fragile, capable of breaking or melting, and even more significant for our purposes here, a phallic version of frigidity, if one thinks of a tortoise as pulling in its phallus-like members for protection to retreat from (sexual) experience. In other words, the opposite of the winged octopi. From first to last, then, not only a dissociation, but also a retraction has occurred. If we look at the third vehicular image, we see that a network is being produced through repetition and difference. "Mon épave, peut-être tu t'y égratineras sans la voir comme on se jette sur une arme flottante." Surely this wreck is the tragic antithesis to the boat guided by the winged octopi, down to its very dismembering, which we must see by now as an image of the subject's castration anxiety. What other textual evidence is there for such a reading?

Within the chiasm are also chasms, menacing breaches that threaten to open up and to engulf: "Des cachots suintera une liqueur plus forte que la mort / Quand on la contemple du haut d'un précipice." Here is a vertiginous view into a compelling yet threatening space, following the Medusa image already referred to. My hypothesis is that, given the symmetry of the pronominal dialectic which structures the "je/tu" as equals, a concomitant designation of the female genitalia echoes the images of phallic equivalents. However, as both are articulated from the masculine point of view, as it were – the woman cannot defend herself – the female sex is designated as an object of ambivalence, indirectly named through figuration, and in this poem, always, in its menacing aspect. Textual reiterations of this metaphorical isotope are found in the image of "la mousse creuse," pointing to an anxiety about the void beyond the fluffiness, and even as a sort of mirror image which the poet holds up to the other in his prediction: "Tu verras l'horizon s'entrouvrir et c'en sera fini tout à coup du baiser de l'espace."

Is it far-fetched to see a pun here on "baiser"? In light of the production of meanings these images have thus far engendered, I hardly think so. In fact, we might say that in the whirling movement of the poem, expanding and contracting with a concentric yet centripetal force, what is pushing the couple "je/tu" apart is precisely that the cosmic coitus will *not* take place because on some unconscious level it is too threatening; it cannot take place, and what takes place instead is cosmic cataclysm and catastrophe. The voice of the poem is trying to cover over this fear of the void by generating a dreamscape which simulates plenitude. Yet it reads like a rebus once we have the key, revealing what it did not even know it was covering.

We can go even further, with the help of intertextual and anagrammatic tools. Fear of castration as wound is reiterated in the text in the "adonide goutte de sang." The blood shed is that of Adonis, who, according to myth, was fatally wounded in a hunt. Venus could not save him from death, only transform the blood and resurrect the beloved as anemone. This echoes the "pêcher en fleurs," with its metonymical hands, a pink version of the blood-red death, and also resonates with the "tu te promèneras avec la vitesse qui commande aux bêtes des bois." Yet if "tu" is the beast which mortally wounds her Adonis, it is also because she is Venus, the goddess of love. The "mons veneris" to which Venus gives her name, that part of the female anatomy which prefigures, points to, promises, or covers the genitals, is associatively present in the "adonide goutte de sang." If, as we have demonstrated, the female sex is as present in its menacing cleft form as the phallus is in versions surmembered, dismembered or retracted, it is also present as a lexeme whose graphs and phonemes are disseminated throughout the text without the word itself ever being fleshed out. "Vagin" may be the hidden anagram in "La Mort rose." The initial "v" is reiterated in twenty-seven words in the poem, alliterating and haunting the text in its dismembered, omnipresent, but unpronounceable form. All the letters needed to complete the lexeme are found in the verse "Mon épAVe, peut-être tu t'y éGratINiras," an unconscious reversal serving a compensatory function in the face of the fear of castration, where it is the woman who is warned against being wounded by the floating member. We might even go so far as to say that the female sexual organ *is* "la mort rose," and that fear of and desire for climax, "la petite mort," releases from that scary place the "cachot," "une liqueur plus forte que la mort."

The state of fusion and the fight against it form the rhythm of this text, provoking consequent images of aggression. If union and communion are not possible because of ambivalence towards the desired object, then onirism gives way to onanism, that noncoincidence of climax, or, worse, to impotence, immobility, desperate sadistic aggression, which is now thoroughly mental, disembodied. This is the reading which the last part of the poem imposes on me:

C'est que j'appartiendrai au vide semblable aux marches
   d'un escalier qui s'appelle *bien en peine*
A toi, les parfums dès lors, les parfums défendus
L'angélique
Sous la mousse creuse et sous tes pas qui n'en sont pas
Mes rêves seront formels et vains comme le bruit de paupières
   de l'eau dans l'ombre
Je m'introduirai dans les tiens pour y sonder la profondeur
   de tes larmes
Mes appels te laisseront doucement incertaine. . . .

"Tu" is left alone with the "parfums défendus," analog for the "liqueur." Once again, "je" and "tu" are reciprocally, symmetrically immobilized, in the images of his steps, "marches" which cannot move, and hers, "pas" which negate themselves. They are symmetrically ambivalent, too, since "tes pas qui n'en sont pas" can be read as protests which aren't. Equal, perhaps, in this failed relationship, but separate now, since they dream apart. His dreams, characterized as formal and vain, repeat an earlier line, "Les échos mouleront seuls tous ces lieux qui furent," poignantly attesting to the poem's own impossible futility. As if in a dream, the woman is being sent off and called back at the same time, responding to a different kind of logic. Her train is frozen yet advances, the star descends (would it be, by some ironic poetic justice, Venus?), but we are left gently uncertain as to whether it is to illuminate or annihilate the already fragile "baggages de sable." The penetrating, intrusive gesture of "Je m'introduirai," meant to measure the other's pain, is one last attempt at futile phallic aggression, and "pour y sonder la profondeur de tes larmes" echoes that compelling yet frightening female container, the pink death. The cosmic, the emotional, the rhetorical and the anatomical are densely woven together in this poem.

We have not even begun to isolate the light isotope in the poem, for example, but a quick enumeration of the images would show a similar ambivalent quality – light is either radiating luminosity, or blinding, whirling lightning: "soleil blanc et noir," "comètes qui foudroient," "pause de l'argent," "pêcher en fleurs," "lustre," "diamant trop taillé," "lumière folle," "luciole," "végétation transparente," "étoile," "tortue de glace." The dynamism of the poem is clearly one in which things rise and descend on the vertical plane, imitating tumescence and detumescence; or where things are immobilized or whirl around out of control in space or on earth on the horizontal plane. As the poem progresses it accelerates – gentleness becomes emptiness, violence gives way to madness, until speed freezes into immobility, suppressing danger but also, perhaps, life. The poem must proceed inexorably towards the future, which is its destruction. The fate that awaits woman is solitude, on the order of the poet's own disappearance. She has come to the end of the line, so to speak, because he has exiled her there, being unable to sustain intimacy without fearing loss of individuality. The star descends like a curtain on a stage scene, leaving her forever "cut off" from everything. The poetic punishment fits the fantasized crime of castration.

At some time between genesis and apocalypse, poised on a precipice between climax and a paroxysm of impotence, "La Mort rose" articulates itself as disarticulation of universe and amorous union. Of the unifying forces in the poem, do we have the right to speak of one which we could call the poet's voice? Elusive as it is rhetorically, we can certainly describe it phenomenologically as a gentle tone attempting to master, to control the violence of death by announcing it to the other, warning her, rehearsing it, which means, in French, "répétition." Yet the voice that enunciates the poem cedes to the voices enunciated in the poem, the "tremblement de ta voix," the "échos" and the "appels" which remain unanswered and unanswerable, degraded versions of a lost plenitude of the word or the couple, whose presence seems actually to undermine the poetic enterprise.

If, at the very center of the poem, we find the hushed utterance "silence et vie," can we not assume that its contrary would be "poésie et mort"? If to speak is to disappear, it is also, in this poem, the last possible link between "je/tu," the last appeal, despite its ambivalence, like Orpheus's to Eurydice. The disjunction between the calm voice and its violent predictions and announcements structures the poem's ambivalent dynamics. In Breton, it is a familiar voice. The one which speaks the failure of love, questions it, confides it. We have heard it in *Nadja* and in *Poisson soluble*.

Notes

1. Michael Riffaterre, "La Métaphore filée dans la poésie surréaliste," in *Langue Française 3* (Paris: Larousse, 1969); Jean Ricardou, *Pour une théorie de nouveau roman* (Paris: Seuil, 1971), and *Le Nouveau roman* (Paris: Seuil, 1973); Julia Kristeva, *Séméiotiké: Recherches pour une sémanalyse* (Paris: Seuil, 1969), and *La Révolution du langage poétique* (Paris: Seuil, 1974); Jean Starobinski, *Les Mots sous les mots* (Paris: Gallimard, 1971); François Rastier, "Systématique des isotopies," in A. J. Greimas, ed., *Essais de sémiotique poétique* (Paris: Larousse, 1972); Emile Benveniste, *Problèmes de linguistique générale* (Paris: Gallimard, 1966); Xavière Gauthier, *Surréalisme et sexualité* (Paris: Gallimard, 1971).

2. See the chapter in Benveniste entitled "L'Homme dans la langue."

Toward a New Definition of Automatism: *L'Immaculée Conception*

Jacqueline Chénieux-Gendron

Les Champs magnétiques, which inaugurated the history of Surrealism, has been the object of numerous critical studies, textual or historical; the historical studies have relied on passages by Breton himself (and by Aragon, the privileged witness) which take stock of the experience, passages written by Breton in 1922 and in 1924, allusions made by Philippe Soupault, and passages, finally, written by Aragon, but these came much later.[1] However, *L'Immaculée Conception (The Immaculate Conception)*, an enigmatic and provocative text penned by Breton and Paul Éluard, is often *invoked* by critics, but has never been the specific object of any study, textual or historical. Until now, the critical gaze has focused only on the *mimesis* of psychotic discourse which, under the title of "Possessions," makes up the second part of the text, preceded by an introduction which testifies to its authenticity; the only important discussion of it was written by André Rolland de Renéville in the *Nouvelle Revue Française* of 1 February 1932:

I do not believe that it is possible to momentarily experience the state of consciousness of a total paralytic if one has not been stricken with the illness oneself. There would have to be, at the very least, a progressive mental destruction which would not allow the man who underwent it to return to his former state.

I will come back to this epistemological naiveté later.

My hypothesis is that, for Surrealism, automatism never ceased to be in process. Rather than envisioning the chronology of the corpus of automatic texts as a sudden and violent blaze (in 1919) which gradually dies down, with secondary fires like those of the period of "sleeps," then *Poisson soluble* and finally *L'Immaculée Conception* and *Ralentir travaux* (Breton, Éluard, Char, 1930); rather than adopting a point of view which would coincide with that of Breton, who in 1929 clearly indicated his disappointment – automatic writing: an "indisputable cliché" – and, in 1933, speaking of the "continuous misfortune" of the automatic message, seems to establish its final moment, I propose to discuss sympathetically the theoretical stakes of these textual exercises, but also to reformulate them without limiting them to petrified and perhaps secondary formulas like that of "dictation of the mind" – a formula advanced by Breton in the *Manifeste* of 1924. Some critics justify these formulas at all costs; others use them to put Breton's thought in contradiction with itself.

It is essential to remember that play is at the center of all surrealist practices. The first automatism, that of *Les Champs magnétiques,* was experienced as an overwhelming dictation by human thought to the hand of a single man. This is the "romantic" period of automatism, where textual "labor" is connected to the creation of a sacred anthology. The final triumphant period of automatism – that of *L'Immaculée Conception* and *Ralentir travaux* – displays much more clearly its playful swiftness. René Char speaks of the three-voiced automatic poems of *Ralentir travaux* as "bundles of kindling, hastily tied up"; Breton and Éluard testify in 1935 to the rapidity with which *L'Immaculée Conception* was written: "The book was written in fifteen days, and in that time we consecrated to it only our hours of *real leisure.*"[2] After 1930, automatism scatters throughout Surrealism and is no longer concentrated in "pure" texts. The year 1930 does mark the final moment of an experiment. But there are endings which are richer than certain beginnings, for this "ending" gives free rein to everything that play can imply in a mentality whose coloration is poetical/magical.

Is *L'Immaculée Conception* an automatic text? How can it be automatic, divided as it is into three large movements of continuous prose ("L'Homme," "Les Possessions," "Les Médiations") and a final, aphoristic segment, "Le Jugement originel"? A knowledge of the protocol which governed this writing *à deux* can give us some clue as to the answer to these questions. Either the pages, written in unrestrained, uncontrollable torrents, were grouped into sections secondarily, or the large movements of the text were decided a priori, with their themes – and this was the case, according to André Breton and Philippe Soupault, with some parts of *Les Champs magnétiques.*

These pages have been illuminated for us by the discovery of two and, exceptionally, even three, levels of manuscripts, which correspond to the near totality of the pages, and which were found in Paris in two different collections. Here, fortune favored me as if what gamblers say about "beginner's luck" were true. This gives us the chance to see "the work in progress." In light of these preliminary texts, abandoned projects and vaguely sketched plans, a textual study can progress. The text thus reveals a large number of its processes of invention and composition: a game of oppositions, mirrors or echoes. The identification of the writers (or transcribers), as indicated on the manuscript which Éluard gave to Nusch, is confirmed. Much more interesting is the acknowledgment that the distinction between *poem* and *automatic writing* loses its sense. These texts have been worked over, but not as a poem by Hugo might be. Rather, the corrections are immediate in the flow of the original draft. They are governed, as well, by rules of writing whose boundaries are established in advance and whose number is limited. That is why we might talk of an automatic *work* rather than automatic writing.

The Work of Automatism Induced by Titles

Our first step will be to examine the text of the manuscript by confronting it with the printed text.[3] The textual device which introduces the successive movements which make up *L'Immaculée Conception* is the series of titles. The working manuscript consists of a number of loose sheets, twenty-one by twenty-seven centimeters, using the back of the imprinted stationery of the hotel Au Rendez-Vous des Artistes in the Parisian suburb of Cernay-la-Ville. This paper, which was used for the chapter titled "L'Homme," conserved in a private collection, permits us to confirm the authenticity of the ulterior chapters, conserved in another, semi-public, collection. To every page written by Breton corresponds a page written by Éluard, in a sequence of small, numbered units, analogous to verses. They are then alternately, and without the numbers, "mounted" on the second manuscript, copied in a larger format (33 × 24.5 cm). On the very first manuscript, then, the titles precede the texts. Do they introduce them or do they induce them? Are they placed there *after* the sequences have been written? This second hypothesis is unconvincing, because the placement of the title, the disposition of the margins of the page, and the handwriting of each author lead to the conclusion that the titles intervene at the origin of the text, like the *la* (as Breton would have said) or its *incipit* (as Aragon will say of his own prose). These titles preside over the pages at three *moments.*

First of all, at the origin of the text, the general title of *L'Immaculée Conception* is given, it seems, in a religious/anti-religious semantic context within which the surrealist group has been working since Dali's arrival in Paris in 1928. With this arrival, preceded by the scandalous renown of the film *Un Chien andalou,* the practice of playful provocation is renewed within the group. Already Max Ernst had used "L'Immaculée Conception" as the title of two plates in the first chapter of his "novel" *La Femme 100 têtes* (1929). The religious semantic field thus defined had scattered to several places in the text. The epigraph of the chapter titled "L'Homme" refers to the Greek name of the Gospel, the "Good News" (Bonne-Nouvelle): "Let's take the Boulevard Bonne-Nouvelle and show it." There is a certain intertextuality at work in this phrase as well, which goes back to the epilogue of *Nadja* and reorients interpretation in the direction of the apology for *disorder* and anarchy.[4] The title "Possessions" in its turn refers to demonology, whose acceptance is secularized without a fundamental change of vector: the authors permit themselves to be inhabited by a succession of delirious consciousnesses without the derisive intention which

Aragon had in publishing *Entrée des succubes* – a part of the *Défense de l'infini*.[5] And "Le Jugement originel" – product of the juxtaposition of the terms "original sin" and "last judgment" – closes the series of the four intermediary titles.

What serves as channel for this religious semantic field is the reformulated Good News, secularized and made immanent, of the new game that guilt, interdiction and the question of engenderment are playing in the surrealist mentality around the matter of textual invention.

The four large movements of the text constitute still another level where the titles play. Three among them correspond to the semantic diapason struck by the general title, but assuredly not the third, "Médiations." "L'Homme" was written just before the three others, and doubtless served as core and model: model for the protocol of writing, model for the length of the texts, model for the construction of the cyclical ensemble. The chapter "L'Homme," almost finished by 27 August 1930,[6] precedes the rapid writing of the rest, which will be published as a whole, and is dated "September 1–15, 1930" on the latest manuscript, recopied but still full of alterations. The allegation of a very rapid writing is corroborated by the ulterior affirmation made by Breton and Éluard in the *Cahiers d'Art* of 1935. The prepublication of this part of the book in a review confirms the impression that "L'Homme" constitutes an entirety in itself in its thematic, cyclical, and uneven construction, which juxtaposes life and death, and distends conception, intrauterine life, and birth to the dimensions of three textual movements. In the same way, Dali's drawings represent a bomb *before* its explosion in the first frame, and in the last, four pages later, the bomb exploding. Life is a bombardment, and the instant of bombardment is thus distended to the dimensions of the text in its entirety, which is placed under an epigraph which lauds the accomplishments of disorder and anarchy, an epigraph which was added to the text with Dali's drawings.

Similarly, in the ensemble of *L'Immaculée Conception*, the final part is presented as an origin ("Le Jugement originel"). Between "L'Homme" and "Le Jugement," "Possessions," with the attempt to simulate a psychotic delirium, and "Médiations" confront each other. I propose to envision in the different chapters which make up these two overall movements the symbolic itinerary of different stations, like the stations of a religious ritual, the "Way of the Cross" for example, in the invention of the poetic word.

The possessions are possessions of the tongue by madness; the mediations, which lead us from "La Force de l'habitude" to "L'Idée du devenir" by way of "La Surprise," "Il n'y a rien d'incompréhensible," "Le Sentiment de la nature," and "L'Amour," emerge from the ethical itinerary undertaken by the "normal" man. The title of "Médiations" seems to have been borrowed from Hegel, whom Breton was rereading in a French translation at the period when he had just finished the *Second Manifeste*.[7] The preface to

The Phenomenology of the Spirit describes mediation as "nothing else than the movement of equality with oneself; in other words, it is reflection in itself, the moment of I being for myself; it is pure negativity or, reduced to its pure abstraction, *simple becoming,*" Finally, it is "Le Jugement originel," where the textual movements regain their aphoristic form (which they employed only in "L'Amour") rather than adopting a lyrical or sarcastic mode in the manner of Lautréamont. The title of this part, which was greatly worked over, turns the phrase "last judgment" inside out and crosses it with the phrase "original sin"; the product of this union is the promise of the absolute: it appears to me to designate the place – mythical if ever place was – where poetic language would be sufficient unto itself, without exterior conditioning, without reference either to madness ("Possessions") or to the norm of a life which is simply lived. Here, Breton's aphorism clashes swords with Éluard's aphorism; the signifier, made rhythmic by a rigid prosody and a repetitive syntax in the imperative mode, produces "sense"; the play of the utterance gives access to the unthought (*impensé*): there, in effect, poetic invention is *judged.*

To the question of the choice of titles for the subsections which constitute these large textual units, and of their role as inducers of writing, the manuscripts give us at least one answer, brilliantly clear and perhaps exemplary for understanding the labor of automatism. Three series of large units are envisaged on a significant page.

1. The two respective pages by Breton and Éluard both bear the general title "Médiations," enumerating in one line the initial possibilities, in four terms: "Woman. Beauty. Knowledge. Justice." These themes are crossed out by both writer/transcribers. This banality, however, will be taken up once more in the condensed formula used to describe the objectives of Surrealism in 1944: "Poetry, liberty and love."[8] This very banality signals the rapidity with which it was written.

2. Whatever the reasons for the abandonment of these themes envisaged for the large units might be, a second series of propositions, which are presented in two successive lines, is then formulated:

The feeling for nature. The sentiment of love.
The idea of justice.
The illusion of progress. Revolutionary hope.

Symmetrical alterations and substitutions by both writers lead to the next formulation in four terms:

The feeling for nature. Love.
"Nothing is incomprehensible." Revolutionary hope.

From the first version to the second, the emergence of the statement "the feeling of nature" is striking. The final text reads:

The procedure of the convex mirror has served more than once to study the [sources of the dew]; when it is completed by [the fire in the hearth], it can be painlessly submitted to precise measurement, and the phenomenon can be studied in all its details. . . .
We would have liked to illustrate this text with a curious figure representing an animal with a long trunk, strangely bifurcated halfway down. The existence of analogous beings is everywhere signalled.[9]

The *nature* in question here is less vegetable than animal, and the feelings are not close to Jean-Jacques Rousseau's: they are, rather, techniques of initiation, or expositions of knowledge relating to animals.[10] From this we can conclude that the pages which served as *pattern* were taken from the journal *La Nature,* which we know was studied closely by the Surrealists, from Max Ernst to André Breton, and whose cover was practically traced (it has identical graphic design and choice of typeface) to produce the bright red cover of *La Révolution surréaliste.*
But the intention of the inducing schema of the "large units" has not yet been sufficiently clarified. It will be revealed to us by a double analogy.
3. The following pages of the rough draft establish a series of six terms, adding to the preceding titles "Surprise" and "Force of habit," placed at the beginning, and arranged by a later numbering thus:

Force of habit. Surprise. Nothing is
incomprehensible.
The feeling for nature. Love. Revolutionary
hope.

These two terms, added on at the originating outposts of writing, have an antithetical relationship, the second ("Surprise") valued by the Surrealists, and the first ("habit") repulsed.
The analogy emerges between the first series of words and the second: in the same way as "Force of habit" is opposed to "Surprise" and to the thematic of "Nothing is incomprehensible," so is "The sentiment of nature," treated derisively by the review *La Révolution surréaliste,* opposed to "Love" and to "Revolutionary hope." In the order of knowledge, the "Force of habit" must be shaken off in favor of the search for (poetic) surprise and of the idea of (revolutionary) progress. In the order of action, the maniacal search for experimentation (which has nothing to do with true knowledge) must be left behind in favor of the quest for love and revolution. The first analogy we have discovered is in effect a mirror which separates the texts of "Médiations" into two series. On the one hand "Surprise" and "Il n'y a rien d'incompréhensible" mimic the inventive efflorescence, and are opposed to "La Force de l'habitude," whose rough drafts reveal the difficulty it presented to mimesis. On the other hand, "L'Amour" and "L'Espoir révolutionnaire" (ultimately titled "L'Idée du devenir") are opposed to "Le Sentiment de la nature," which is weighty and derivative.
The second analogy brings us back to the outline of the large units

which make up "Possessions." Among the five attempts at simulation, the four last are deliriums imitating profound psychoses which were favorably received by the Surrealists: "La Manie aiguë," whose title in the drafts was "maniacal-depressive psychosis," pours out a lyrical hymn, slightly modulated by an imaginative depression; "La Paralysie générale," as its first readers quickly perceived,[11] is a magnificent hymn to love; "Délire d'interprétation," far from being the paranoia which hypertrophies the reasoning faculties and which usually focuses on the minuscule details of daily life, offers us a hallucinatory reverie describing an overhanging delirium; "La Démence précoce," also called "flight of ideas," allows the mind to flee in onomatopoeic syllables, but not without first displaying the beauty of a continuous and image-laden utterance, only slightly different from that of the "Paralysie générale" section. "Essai de simulation de la débilité mentale," on the contrary, precedes and contradicts this lyrical majority, offering us a series of moral clichés, and is marked by an anxiousness to be respected.

The Work of Automatism as a Game of Magic: The Ritual of Correction

The second characteristic I would like to point out is the *clannish* activity which is manifested through this double-voiced text. The fact that the duality of writings is concealed must be taken into consideration: the prepublication of "L'Homme," like the original publication, does not permit the reader to distinguish the parts written by Breton from those written by Éluard. The game of "recognizing" stylistic traits can be played at length. Even Aragon in "L'Homme coupé en deux" was mistaken about the identity of the writers of *Les Champs magnétiques.* Who could have been closer to Breton and Soupault than Aragon, even though he was not in Paris during the spring of 1919? In addition to this textual unification, which offers the reader long bursts of writing with no indentation (or brief aphorisms, in "L'Amour" and "Le Jugement originel") and above all without any indication of whose hand held the pen, the manuscript given to Nusch by Éluard (several years after the text was written) distinguishes with irreproachable exactness the voice of the one from the voice of the other. Moreover, it seems probable that Éluard based this scrupulous identification less on his memory than on the working manuscript. The evidence is convincing that it was during the thirties that Éluard, in need of money, sold the major part of this working manuscript to Picasso, in whose collection we were able to find it.

The entity which is being formed here is the surrealist "voice," identified by the joint signature "Breton-Éluard." The absence of divisions, distinctions, or ruptures between the two textual masses is already apparent on the second manuscripts: when Breton and Éluard "mount" their text, alternating the small units of the one with those of the other, recopied carefully by hand within a larger format, preserved in Picasso's archives, the two handwritings are distinct from each other but they appear on a single page. Printing then effaces all the distinctions. The problem of the literary ownership of these texts is posed, as it is for the ensemble of the automatic corpus. Is it then a question of knowing to whom belongs "the voice of our unconscious," as Breton very rightly said in "Entrée des mediums"? A page of the rough draft described above gives, under the mark of one or the other of the writer/transcribers, a breakdown of the number of sections. Were they already trying to plan for the distribution of royalties? Such an idea is absurd, since the "surrealist publishers" brought out only texts which were published "at the author's expense," under the auspices of the publisher José Corti. This page simply shows that Breton and Éluard, wanting to publish the texts of L'Immaculée Conception, quickly calculated the number of pages which were to be published at their expense.

Does the act of publication have a bearing on the secret modalities of invention? Most assuredly it does. And even more than one might think, for it seems clear to me that even Salvador Dali's role as illustrator is implicated in the writing of L'Immaculée Conception. Dali, who is far from Cernay-la-Ville between September 1 and September 15, 1930, living with Gala—to whom Éluard writes assiduously—is the privileged witness: the person to whom these pages are written.

This affirmation might appear paradoxical, and deserves clarification. "L'Ane pourri," the first text by Dali to be published in a surrealist magazine,[12] is still recent. It has quickly assumed the status of a manifesto. Published contiguously with Breton's superb prologue "Il y aura une fois," Dali's pages differentiate themselves from automatism, which is described as a passive state among others. This could not have failed to sting Breton. The paranoical-critical activity which Dali proposed was presented as an active game between the graphic signified and the possible signifiers. The game begins at the signified and returns to it, through the medium of two signifiers, between which an analogy takes place. An African hut can be read as the profile of a face when its photograph is turned vertically. Everything happens as if Breton, with Éluard's support, had accepted this challenge, and proposed an active mimesis of certain psychotic deliriums. Dali would thus be the privileged recipient of the text. This intuition is plausible, though not, strictly speaking, provable. An amusing piece of evidence for it is provided by a collage (perhaps accidental) in the rough draft: when Breton and Éluard recopied "L'Homme" for publication in S.A.S.D.L.R. (the recopied pages are preserved in the private collection where I consulted them), they indicate in the margin the typographical style they want, and, as an example to insure that their instructions will be followed by the typographer, they glue a fragment of

Dali's article onto the page. Additionally and most important, Dali is the artist who is asked to sketch the illustrations for this prepublication. I have already mentioned that these illustrations were directly related to the epigraph of the chapter "L'Homme," an epigraph of a revolutionary and anarchist orientation which does not appear in the first drafts. Finally, according to Georges Hugnet, the insert ("prière d'insérer") to the published version of *L'Immaculée Conception* was written by Dali (it matters little whether Dali, in 1930, was able to employ the perfect French formulations we read, or whether the "prière d'insérer" was in its turn "corrected" by Éluard or Breton.[13] The "prière d'insérer" emphasizes "the power which the mind has of successively adopting all the modalities of madness." The *power* is emphasized, and not the passivity, of automatism.

Rather than speaking of a *fusion* between Breton and Éluard in a brotherhood of writing, I will speak of a reciprocal *correction* which might even go three ways, between Breton, Éluard and Dali.

In certain respects, it is the absent Dali who controls the production of this text, who then illustrates and orients the first part, and finally who proclaims the validity of the experience in writing the "prière d'insérer." We know also that the signifier *correction* – in all senses of the term – had slipped into the practices and the allusions of the Surrealists during those years. Does it not appear in the title of Ernst's painting *The Virgin Correcting the Infant Jesus before Three Witnesses, André Breton, Paul Éluard and the Author* (1926), and in one of the aphorisms of "Le Jugement originel" ("Correct your parents")? Does it not appear as well in the imperious figure of Gala?

Correction, thus, is an initiatic rite. Reciprocal correction is permitted, admitted and desired among the members of a clan. It is the product of the leisures of an elect group.

Textual correction is also an issue here. On the two levels of rough drafts we have described, the initial outburst of writing is conserved, though it is modified and perturbed in two very different ways. After the first outburst, which is numbered in sequences or small units, sections of the rapidly written text are marked out; interlinear corrections are added; and sometimes, though rarely, entire sequences are done away with. The recopied pages take these corrections into account and add others, after the "Essai de simulation du délire d'interprétation" ("Possessions," chapter 4). These corrections become more substantial with the attempt at simulation of dementia praecox, but after the third chapter of "Médiations" ("Il n'y a rien d'incompréhensible") the small format is missing. The intervening chapters are fragments of new beginnings or very marked-up rough drafts, placed directly on the larger format. The first thing which can be concluded from this is that the absence of preliminary drafts on the smaller paper is unfortunate; under the impetus of the first outburst, Éluard and Breton permit themselves to employ a different protocol for writing: by turns, they use the same paper. The second conclusion is that here correction took the form of a change of the inventive technique when the authors were not satisfied with the quality of the text.

An unpublished page, written in both hands, appears under the title "Il n'y a rien d'incompréhensible," which was certainly borrowed from Lautréamont. This aphorism is often cited or played with by the Surrealists. But neither Éluard nor Breton was taken with phlegmatic irony. It is only with the third sequence, written by Breton, that, with the theme of the city, the theme of the murder of passion emerges: "Moreover, two days do not pass without a murder of passion." Éluard takes his turn with the pen, but the line is interrupted in the middle of a phrase, after the clause: "There is in the . . . ." This abandoned page can be understood as the springboard for the long, fantastic, and frenetic narration which was recopied and published as we know it. It is in reality an altered "readymade" or a playful collage which in its original form had appeared in the newspaper *L'Intransigeant* (11 September 1930), which refers to the prestigious concert of Vladimir Horowitz and says: "What attraction has brought together on an Alpine plateau at a thousand meters above Sierre some of the greatest musical performers of our time," now changed to: "What attraction has thus brought together at the bottom of this abyss, a thousand meters below sea level, several of the greatest criminals of our time?" – the beginning of the text published under the title "Il n'y a rien d'incompréhensible."

"Il n'y a rien d'incompréhensible" extends the attempt at comprehension of certain psychoses to criminality as well. Another unpublished page can be connected to this frenetic attempt: "Each of them drinks a bowl of the other's blood. The bowl is a marvelously lunar color and every evening a sweeter lull follows the useless, the adorable sacrifice."

After the deceptive and sarcastic chapter titled "Le Sentiment de la nature," the chapter called "L'Amour" again is corrected from beginning to end. Several "throw-outs" have remained in the rough drafts: one by Breton followed by Éluard, the other by Éluard alone. Both are written in a lyrical mode which is characterized by a certain banality:

The secret love is contained in these words: it must always be the first time. . . . The admirable other side of this beautiful secret is contained in these words: it must always be the last time [Breton's hand].

A slight liberty taken by the man's tenderness towards the woman into whose eyes he gazes and that's it for all that those eyes were so badly defending [Éluard's hand].

It is at that stage, it seems, that Breton and Éluard, unsatisfied, sought an entirely different mode of writing, which is that of a non-parodying rewriting of the various positions of love, alternately based on the syntactic and semantic model of the Kama Sutra and on the thematic model of popular tradition. In doing this, Éluard certainly must have remembered the text which he wrote with Max Ernst in *Littérature*, "And According to Your Case."[14] Éluard and Breton are thus "correcting" the Kama Sutra; they are "correcting" popular tradition; they are "correcting" themselves.

But all this takes place, finally, as if correction had become possible and permissible because the phrase which acted as springboard had been "incorporated." It is Breton who brings up the word "incorporate" in regard to the half-sleeping phrase in the *Manifeste* of 1924: "Immediately I could only think of incorporating it into the material of my poetic construction." The term "incorporation" has magical connotations. It generalizes the ritual of ingestion, which induces a transformation of the being and a more extensive or more intense sacred power. It is as if the "given" phrase, once *incorporated,* acts to *guarantee* the automatic outburst (by instigating the play of harmonics evoked by Breton in the simple title *Le La,* 1961) or, alternately, to *guarantee* the disruptions of static forms that can be found in "L'Amour," and then in "Le Jugement originel." In this last chapter, which is abundantly corrected (we have three rough drafts, each with a greatly differing number of aphorisms), almost all of these short forms employ an imperative syntax. We have not found a pattern in these new-fangled proverbs, which make up the *vers dorés* of a surrealist consciousness: the same proverbial rhythm, the same ethical topics. But neither the number of precepts (71 in the classic translation by Fabre d'Olivet of the text attributed to Pythagoras; 59 or 78, depending on the draft, in "Le Jugement originel"), nor the formal precision, nor the thematics are truly "contested" or upset by Éluard and Breton: the opposite approach to the one they had both just taken in December 1929 in "Notes sur la poésie," which upset the poetic precepts of Valéry printed in *Commerce.*

Here, the work of writing is classical. Paradoxes are sent out in all directions, emerging from the slippage from signifier to signifier, or from signified to signified. For example, the twenty-eighth aphorism – "Sell something to eat, buy something to starve to death" – had first been suggested by the banal phrase "Buy something to eat . . ."; the emergence of "Sell something to die" provokes the more paradoxical semantic inversion. Another slippage of signifieds is "Don't flinch, it's pain" – a good stoic precept which is revealing also in respect to Breton; under his pen it becomes "Without flinching, form a possible idea of swallows." If the "Notes sur la poésie" constituted an "art poétique" for Surrealism, "Le Jugement originel," in a complementary movement, first proposes a surrealist ethics: in defense of the quest, not the capture (twentieth aphorism); in defense of availability (second), of the powers of childhood (fourth), of dreams (seventh), violence (tenth), chance (forty-fifth), becoming in itself ("Write the imperishable on sand"), etc.

Automatic Work as the Play of Stereotypes

In "Possessions," Éluard and Breton enter into a debate over the problem which Aragon had already posed in "Une Vague de rêves": "To simulate something, is this any different from thinking it? And what is thought, is."[15]

The authors hope, they say, "to prove that the spirit, *poetically* trained within the normal man, is capable of reproducing in its largest features the most paradoxical and eccentric verbal manifestations . . ." (introduction to "Médiations"). "Possession" by the evil spirit does not induce an enduring problem; the possessed possesses: "The spirit has the power to submit the principal delirious ideas to its will without causing an enduring problem for itself." The ideas do not possess it; it submits them to its purposes.

This entire introduction, which is written in Breton's hand on the manuscript, accentuates poetic *training* – a strained and difficult exercise which puts all of the (poetic) resources of human inventiveness into play.

Critics, however (mainly André Rolland de Renéville), have acted as if the alternative were this: either, wanting to imitate a delirium, one allows oneself to be invaded by the delirium; one reproduces in its experiential totality a state of consciousness capable of producing the verbal outbursts which characterize this state – and this in the absence of any clinical and psychiatric information: it would thus be something like a hypnotic state; or else, one intellectually simulates a discourse after having analyzed a typical one whose authenticity is guaranteed, and then, by placing its elements side by side, finally reconstructs the scaffolding. In this case, one would be creating a pastiche. This alternative is clearly imagined by Rolland de Renéville in his article of 1 February 1932, which I cited at the beginning of this essay. After having placed the authenticity of "possession" in doubt ("There would have to be, at the very least, a progressive mental destruction which would not allow the man who underwent it to return to his former state"), he adopts the other, contradictory hypothesis:

I persist in the belief that these pages of *L'Immaculée Conception* could only have been obtained through the effort of a very well informed research of the verbal forms produced by the various mental deliriums, and a deliberate decision to simulate the discourses which correspond to these deliriums.[16]

André Breton does not contradict this in his letter to Rolland de Renéville of February 1932.[17] But he clarifies and discusses three points: first, he challenges the validity of the alternative in which he is locked (intellectual pastiche *or* irreversible state of consciousness); then he makes the notion of automatic work more explicit. He proves, in effect, that it is a question of putting a good face on bad luck. Since it is known that automatism is always more or less arranged as a poem, this direction/determination must be dealt with by an inversion of its place:

What could be more *tempting,* consequently, than to substitute this determination which is specifically ours with a determination of another order, whatever that might be, and as strange as you wish, provided that the words are not made to gravitate around their circle *for nothing?* It appeared to us that this determination could, for example, very well be the groups of symptoms diagnosed today as the pathology of one mental disease or another. Thus conditioned, the unknown word . . .[18]

This phrase is of capital importance. It deals with the *conditions* of writing, and of the demonstration of these conditions to the writer/transcriber. In the same way as for *Les Champs magnétiques* the speed of the writing and the semantic themes were imposed on the writing beforehand, here the knowledge of the primary features of specific symptoms of certain diseases of the word can be taken as the point of departure of an active mimesis. Thus Breton shows with great intuitive certainty that the disorders of language can be formalized (this is the third point of his response). It is even easier to imitate a delirious discourse than to imitate a poetic utterance. It is certainly easier to delineate the parameters laid down to "construct" an utterance linked by stereotype and disease than to delineate or perceive intuitively the parameters laid down to "construct" a so-called normal language. "We knew," Breton wrote with beautiful intuition, "that thought can only use a small number of alarm signals to manifest its most extreme problems."[19]

In his letter of 1932 to Rolland de Renéville, Breton redefines the very notion of pastiche as an *economy:* "What would happen if these signals were manipulated at will, in relatively autonomous groups, corresponding to the modes of connection revealed by psychiatric analysis?"[20] It must be said that the authority of several psychiatrists confirmed him, in a more precise description of the experience of automatism. J. Lévy-Valensi, P. Migault and Jacques Lacan had just reaffirmed, in an article in the *Annales médico-psychologique,* the interest for psychiatry of the Surrealists' automatic works, the role of the *game,* and the role of *intention* in these exercises.[21]

Breton and Éluard, who were well acquainted with psychiatric nosology, used the classic classifications as they were described by Emile Kraepelin in a book which had been available in French since 1907 and which Breton had been reading since 1916. He had also read Valentin Magnan and was acquainted with Freud's work, first through Regis's accounts, and then directly, as it was translated into French during the twenties. Without this knowledge of psychiatric nosology, Breton and Éluard would not have tried to reproduce specific symptoms; they would have counterfeited "madness" as a vulgar poser might try to ape it. Furthermore, the idea of a systematic attempt at simulation, for poetic reasons, could not have emerged until psychiatric nosology itself had been constituted through the work of Kraepelin and Magnan.

As for the choice of deliriums, it responds to certain intentions whose broad outlines can be traced. The principle has already been indicated: the first attempt at simulation, that of mental debility, is the deceptive and ridiculous obverse of the simulations of great, imaginative psychoses which follow it. These last four are placed by Breton and Éluard, and not without a certain artifice, in the context of great imaginative lyricism. The first ("Essai de simulation de la manie aiguë") is for the most part euphoric and hyperrhythmic, despite the three first phrases and especially the last paragraph, which, at the two boundaries of the text, make evident the fundamental disorder onto which the gaudy and clownish discourse of the maniac is grafted. Material for the second delirium, that of total paralysis, was not lacking in the various works which we are sure were read by André Breton; but the depressive tendency, which Kraepelin describes beside the delusions of grandeur, is left out in favor of the expression of the delusions of grandeur; and finally the thematic of this delirium of grandeur is displaced by the authors' usual themes of philanthropy, altruism, prodigality, which they move towards the discourse of mad love. As for the phenomenon of paranoia, it exercised a great fascination on the Surrealists at this time (Dali's article "L'Ane pourri" had just come out), but it is interesting to note that among the two forms of the delirium traditionally distinguished by Kraepelin (the delirium of interpretation and the delirium of persecution), it is the first which is privileged by the Surrealists; or, rather, instead of simulating an interpretative delirium focused on the minuscule details of daily life, Breton and Éluard transcribe the thought processes of a chronic paranoiac who believes himself to be a bird, thus poeticizing the process of identification. A plethora of novel images emerges from this, as well as a coherence in the delirium of metamorphosis into a bird which might give rise to certain reservations, and which did give rise to some described by Breton in his letter to Rolland de Renéville.

Finally, as regards *dementia praecox*—so extensively studied by Constanza Pascal and by Kraepelin, and designated by Bleuler in 1911 as "a group of schizophrenias"—the attempt at its simulation is easily accomplished by Breton and Éluard, who limit themselves to a synthesis of the symptoms which generally emerge over a long period of time. The disintegration of the mental faculties is accelerated: a myth of schizophrenia rather than a simulacrum of any one schizophrenic state, but one where echolalia—"Neisser's syndrome," when the patient, intoxicated by a word which erupts in the middle of the conversation, repeats it incessantly—and paraphrasia—Ganser's syndrome, a problem with coordinating the linguistic apparatus, typified by responses which are "beside the question"—and all the other neologisms can be recognized.

The choices are, then, oriented towards the psychoses whose discourse tends to be of an expressive and creative type, and when certain symptoms are divergent, the text moves subtly towards those same tendencies.

Automatism, in its ultimate phase, thus presents itself as an activity of leisure different from what it was for *Les Champs magnétiques*. And still the playful attitude must be distinguished from hoax: when Desnos publishes an article signed by Éluard entitled "Le Genie sans miroir," in *Les Feuilles libres* in 1924, where he interweaves his own texts with phrases issued from a delirium, he does it with the intention of demonstrating the incompetence of Wieland Mayr, general secretary of *Feuilles libres*, as a reader, and also in the spirit of provoking all those who assimilate surrealist texts with the works of madmen. This spirit of play implies a poetical engagement of the mind in its entirety, but also an acute perception of the inanity of the goals which offer themselves to our will. In this form, the spirit of play belongs to the magical mentality whose rituals employ this possession/dispossession of the self. This is why I have pointed out here the connections which are woven between (playful) writing and clannish activity: in order to constitute a clan, there must be at least three members, and I see the third man as Salvador Dali.

Moreover, automatism in *L'Immaculée Conception* no longer presents itself at all as the mind's dictation. A "small number of alarm signals" (we might generalize this as "parameters"), according to Breton, make up the "frame" in which the writer/transcribers place themselves. This search for a parameter was effectively present from the first moment of writing, since the rough drafts allow us to see the inducing role of the titles, and the contempt for the first attempt, if it did not correspond to the intention, as was the case with the entire page of "Nothing is incomprehensible," which was abandoned.

But finally, we must return to the spirit of play, which Breton and Éluard establish in the relationship between their enterprise and psychiatric knowledge, or even between their enterprise and Freud's intentions. As regards the knowledge of psychiatrists, the challenge is patent, and is backed up by literary history (in November 1929 the *Annales médico-psychologiques* report the repercussions of the ongoing quarrel among the members of the society of the same name instigated by the provocation of *Nadja;* and in the second number of *S.A.S.D.L.R.*, the same issue in which the chapter "L'Homme" appears, Breton's response to this report is published under the title "Mental Medicine Confronted with Surrealism"). As regards Freud, the challenge is less obvious. It seems to me, however, that it is irrefutable for, in the *Second Manifeste*, Breton cites Freud's recently translated *Five Lectures on Psychoanalysis:* "The man who is energetic, and who succeeds ('who succeeds': I leave, of course, the responsibility for this vocabulary to Freud), is he who is able to transmute the fantasies of desire into realities."[22] The reservations regarding the function of the cure are overcome by an unreserved approval of the mechanism described by Freud, as if Breton and Éluard were imitating this "transmutation," with an intention that does not converge with Freud's. Besides the consideration of the *unknown* constituted by psychosis, the reproduction of symptoms for a mechanism which is analogous to that of hysteria thumbs its nose at the effects of the Freudian cure. The celebration by Aragon and Breton of "The Fiftieth Anniversary of Hysteria" finds its fullest expression and its resting place in *L'Immaculée Conception* – as *Poisson soluble* followed the explanations of the first *Manifeste*.

Fabricate to understand, a principle inherited from Leonardo da Vinci, is here very close to *fabricate to master* the magical mentality. Within Surrealism, the collective automatic text is not the product of a romantic fusion of consciousnesses, but the playful production of a tiny initiatic society, reduced to three members.

Translated by Esther Allen

Notes

1. André Breton, "Entrée des mediums," *Littérature,* new series, no. 6 (1 November 1922), reprinted in *Les Pas perdus.* Philippe Soupault alludes to this period in the two largely autobiographical works, *Le Bon apôtre* (1923) and *Histoire d'un blanc* (1927), and Aragon in "L'Homme coupé en deux," *Les Lettres françaises,* no. 1233 (May 1968).

2. See *Cahiers d'Art* 5-6 (1935), 137. Emphasis mine.

3. The chapter "L'Homme" was first printed in *Le Surréalisme A.S.D.L.R.,* no. 2 (October 1930), 10-14, without mention of a larger ensemble of texts, under the joint signature of Breton and Éluard, with a frieze of sketches signed by Salvador Dali, 1930. The ensemble of the other parts was published by the "Editions Surréalistes" in November, under the title *L'Immaculée Conception.* Our references are to the Pléiade edition of Éluard's works, *Oeuvres complètes* (Paris: Gallimard, 1968), I, 305-56.

4. The epilogue written during the winter of 1927-28 alludes to Boulevard Bonne-Nouvelle, Paris, which is said to be "one of those important strategic points I am seeking relating to the question of disorder." In fact on 8 August 1927, a day of general strike, the Boulevard was used as the scene of the struggle. There were demonstrations on behalf of the anarchists Sacco and Vanzetti, who were about to be executed.

5. See *La Revolution surréaliste* 6 (1926).

6. Paul Éluard, *Lettres à Gala* (Paris: Gallimard, 1984), 122. The letter is dated 27 August 1930.

7. The radio interviews with André Parinaud in 1952 give evidence of Hegel's importance for Breton at the time of the *Second Manifeste* (*Entretiens* [Paris: Gallimard, 1969], 151-52); the text of the *Second Manifeste* itself is full of references to the recent French translations of Hegel's works.

8. At the end of *Arcane 17,* written in Canada in 1944, published in New York in 1945.

9. "Le Sentiment de la nature," beginning and page 342. I place the units of substitution which embellish the initial pattern between brackets.

10. See my book *Le Surréalisme et le roman* (Lausanne: L'Age d'Homme, 1983), 105-6. Rousseau is opposed to Sade, who is preferred.

11. Jean Cassou, 10 January 1931, in *Les Nouvelles littéraires,* and immediately after him, Francis de Miomandre, in *L'Européen,* 14 January.

12. *S.A.S.D.L.R.* 1 (July 1930).

13. Here is the "prière d'insérer":

   If the first and second manifestos were the exposition of the manifest content of the surrealist dream, *L'Immaculée Conception* is the exposition of its latent content.

   The original desire to simulate deliriums, systematized or not, has not only the appreciable advantage of giving rise to unforeseen and entirely new poetic forms, but also the transcendent effect of consecrating, in an exemplarily didactic way, the free categories of thought which culminate in mental alienation.

   L'Immaculée Conception will remain the experimental source to which we must return in order to recognize the power of thought to adopt successively all of the modalities of madness: the recognition of this power amounts to an admission of the reality of this madness and an affirmation of its existence. . . .

14. *Littérature,* new series, 7 (December 1922).

15. "Une Vague de rêves" (1924), reedited in *Oeuvres poétiques,* II, 239.

16. André Rolland de Renéville, "Dernier état de la poésie surréaliste," *Nouvelle Revue Française* (1 February 1932), 288.

17. Breton's letter is dated 2 February 1932 and was published in *Nouvelle Revue Française* (1 July 1932), together with Rolland de Renéville's answer.

18. Ibid., 152.

19. Ibid.

20. Ibid.

21. J. Lévy-Valensi, P. Migault, and J. Lacan, "Ecrits 'inspirés': schizographie," *Annales médico-psychologiques* 5 (December 1931), 508–22.

22. *Manifestes surréalistes* (Paris: Gallimard, 1972), 119.

Linkings and Reflections: André Breton and His Communicating Vessels

Mary Ann Caws

> I hate the world and its distractions.
> André Breton, *Les Vases communicants.*

Les Vases communicants, or *The Communicating Vessels* (1932), is an extraordinary book of possibility and impossibility. It wishes to confer, by its magical and yet controlled discourse, a constant expansion upon the world as we know it, through the incessant communication of everything as we experience and have not yet experienced it. At its center there lies the principal image of the dream as the enabling "capillary tissue" between the exterior world of facts and the interior world of emotions, between reality and, let us say, the imagination. The central image of communicating vessels is taken from a scientific experiment of the same name, where a gas passes from one side to the other: the passing back and forth between these two modes is shown to be the basis of surrealist thought, of surreality itself.

Personifying these modes are the two imagined figures of sleep and wakefulness, the sleeping one immobile at the center of the living whirlwind: "Removed from the contingencies of time and place, he really appears to be the pivot of this whirlwind itself, the supreme mediator," and the wakeful one immersed in that fog which is the "density of the things immediately perceptible when I open my eyes."[1] They represent the communicating vessels of interior vision and exterior fact, of night and day, "unreal" and "real."

The universe of the book is full of nomenclature, of detail, of time and place markers, of reference. De Chirico, Nosferatu the Vampire, Huysmans, Hervey, Marx, Feuerbach, Freud, and other heroes people the pages together with a running commentary on the "marvelous" of everyday life, including the relation between the dreamed and the found, in such places as gambling joints like the Eden-Casino, and some boulevards in Paris like the Boulevard Magenta.

"Human love is to be rebuilt like the rest; I mean it can, it must be built on new bases." This belief, like the relation between inner and outer lives, links the present volume closely to *L'Amour fou* and to *Arcane 17*, which are, in the main, books concerning love and the problem of its relation to the outside world. The three books communicate with each other, with the manifestoes, and with *Nadja*, the great tale of the mad woman loved and abandoned.

Working through the Vessels

Among Breton's works, *Les Vases communicants* is the most "philosophical" and "political," in the strong senses of those terms. Upon its theories, the whole edifice of Surrealism, as Breton conceived it, is based. Without its support, the manifestoes and the critical essays, from the collection entitled *La Clé des champs* on, would have lacked scope as well as central focus.

That it has taken so long for these communicating vessels to reach more than a limited number of readers is no great surprise: this work has neither the tragic density of *Nadja* nor the intense lyricism of *L'Amour fou*. It is not centered on the work of artists and writers familiar to a wider public. It is unique unto itself, with its dreams, its high problematization of political comportment, its speculation as to the role of the writer and the artist, and its very deep melancholy.

What does this work desire, we might ask? What does an André Breton want?[2] The answer is, as he says life is, impossible. He wants the things he loves not to hide all the others from him; he wants the strawberries in the woods to be there for him alone, and for all the others; he wants to take history into account and go beyond it; he wants, above all, to be persuasive, even as his style is progressively more difficult, his thought more unfamiliar. He wants Freud, Marx, Kant, alchemy, and the entire history of ideas to be summed up and available. He wants. . . .

And yet indeed the whole history of Surrealism is here, in these pages. With its heartaches and quixotic endeavors, its pangs of conscience and its genuine wish to communicate, the desire itself aimed at such an image as that of communicating vessels is, without qualification, without reservation, enormously moving. What Breton seeks, or tries to have us undertake, is the replacement of the center at the center, the replacement of the person at "the heart of the universe," where, abstracted from those daily events that would decompose integrity into fragmentation, the human personality itself becomes "for all the sorrow and joy external to it, an indefinitely perfectible place of resolution and echo" (p. 198). What endeavor more poetic? How to reconcile it with what we call a political reality?

The image of the communicating vessels was already present within the pages of *Surrealism and Painting* of 1928. It had to wait until *Les Vases com-*

municants to acquire its working out in relation to Marxist theory, and much more.

Defining, or, yet again, redefining Surrealism in these pages, after the unworkable and temporary definition based on automatic writing, Breton formulates the theory of the link (that will later be condensed into the image of the *point sublime,* connecting life to death, up to down, here to there . . .). "I hope," he says of the surrealist movement he is developing,

that it stands as having tried nothing better than to lay down a *conducting wire* between the far too separated worlds of waking and sleeping, of exterior and interior reality, of reason and madness, of a peaceful knowing and love, of life for life and the revolution, etc. (p. 116)

The very notion of the "etc." posed here seems to stretch out the linking notion into the wide spatiality of the text and the world beyond. Breton adds, troubled no doubt by the relation of the poetics of his movement to the politics of the day, by the gap between what we wish for and what we see, his strongest statement in defense of the experiment Surrealism wanted, at its best, to carry out:

At least we will have tried, even if in vain, tried in any case, not to leave any question without an answer and we will have cared about the consistency of the answers we gave. Supposing this terrain to have been ours, was it really of so little merit that we should have abandoned it? (p. 116)

Dream, he repeats, must be mingled with action, unlike the notion of some literary dreamers for whom the former world alone is suitable, and unlike the notion of some political thinkers for whom the pragmatic world alone counts. The true power, lyrical and efficacious, should result from a communication of one with the other. Thus the tripartite structure of the book: first, the case for the linking of the time and space of the dream to those of the world about us. Then, his illustrations, from his own experience, of the quite remarkable workings of "le hasard objectif" or objective chance as the visible and always surprising link of one world to the other, by chance and by some sort of interior necessity. With this is intertwined a sort of disquisition on the place of love in the universe, the revolutionary character of anti-bourgeois feeling as it takes on and conquers the platitudes of bourgeois existence. Just as important to note is that Breton's point of view about traditional religion is unqualified: religion has no place in this newly communicating universe. Humanity takes up the central place, and no mysticism will avail. The final part takes up the relationship of the individual to others, of the poet to other people, and of the revolutionary future to the present as we see it.

As for the dreams Breton tells, he is careful, even as he applies a sort of Freudian schema to them, to point out Freud's own weaknesses, particularly in separating the psychic from the material, and in his own case, stopping short his analysis. Breton shows, at some length, the relation of his own dreams to everyday life, the similar structure in each, and how each works toward the "reconstitution" of himself, once the links are analyzed.

Persistently, the identical question recurs: how to justify the place we take up? how to work out one's position of freedom or – to some extent – solitude in relation to the coupled universe where, placidly, two by two, the others have all chosen others? ("One day in haste, and there was no more question of their being able to separate. No second thoughts" [p. 112]). The intense hatred of claustrophobia is made evident here and the isolation of the speaker at once proud and anguished ("I repeat I was alone" [p. 113]).

But again, the plurality so desired ("in which, in order to dare to write, I must at once lose and find myself") is problematic, precisely in its submerging of the self. Now the comradeship between the Surrealists is to replace that massing of the ordinary crowds because neither the prose of the everyday nor the poetry of dream suffices. Dream has to be replaced in everyday life, and life has to take on some of the qualities of dream. And he includes his optimism: "Resignation is not written on the moving stone of sleep."

And yet, "this time I live in, this time unhappily ebbs away, taking me with it." As Surrealism refuses to posit any end to its revolution, it sees itself in the future – but in the present, the work toward the transformation of the universe has not always the clearest of ways. Obscurity must play a part, even at the lyrically future end of this volume, where truth, with her hair streaming in light, appears at the dark window, to join the contraries, to have the vessels communicate, now and – in Breton's view – forever.

Of Justification: Breton, Freud, and a Pickle

> . . . il y a là une porte entr-ouverte, au-delà de laquelle il n'y a plus qu'un pas à faire pour, au sortir de la maison vacillante des poètes, se retrouver de plain-pied dans la vie
>
> (Les Vases communicants, p. 11)
>
> (. . . there is a door, half-opened, on the other side of which just one step has to be taken, in leaving the shaky house of poets, to find oneself squarely within life.)

Involved in a book about dreams, and yet about daily life, persuaded that there is some communication between night and day, the mysterious and the "real," Breton concerns himself actively with the setting of his adventure of the mind. He could have given to *Les Vases communicants* the subtitle that Kierkegaard gave to his brief and unforgettably complicated *Repetition,* that is, *An Adventure in Experimenting Psychology.* Breton's book sets its venturing, unerringly, between two key figures, the opening one, "the Marquis of Hervey-Saint-Denys, translator of Chinese poetry from the Tang period and the author of an anonymous work that appeared in 1867 under the title *Dreams and the Ways to Guide Them: Practical Observations,* a work that has become sufficiently rare for neither Freud nor Havelock Ellis – both of whom mention it specifically – to have succeeded in finding it" (p. 10), and the closing one, again Freud, this time in relation to himself.

From the opening to the concluding appendix, with an exchange between the founder of dream psychology and the founder of Surrealism, the communication establishes itself as being about work, dreams, and writing, about the writing of letters and of dreams and of a text that will be a linking one, arguing the importance of such links, their precedence and their following. The whole enterprise, the psychological-literary-personal adventure, is located in mind and world and text, at once modestly and knowingly, knowing its own importance, and staking out its claims with care, between its founding figures.

I want to look here at two moments of particular sensitivity, moments that deal with founding and feeling, and that turn on the issues of *justification,* of self and of the other, and of the relation between them. The first is the concluding moment, with the Freud-Breton exchange, nominally about another name, but really about the relation of Surrealism to Freud, of dreams to the dream-father, and his to his. Freud will bring up and bring up again the issue of justification (and the issue of fathering and its relation to his work).

The second, lying in the center of the work of Breton, is, again, about relations and justification, and is deeply troubling along both lines, as troubling, possibly, as it is honest. It will turn out to be about the issue of the room Breton, or any of us, takes up in the world, of necessity. Not about finding or founding a room of one's own, not about the space and time and means for writing – the sort of issue many of us are still dealing with – but rather about the general and specific justification for being here at all. What are we to do with our lives even as we make them into texts, albeit texts of the marvelous lived out? What role has the mind in the world? Of what importance are we to the Other, for whom our work may or may not be of some avail? Breton's central question, crucial as it is, could well be posed for us all.

Looking at Letters

The appendix, with its three letters from Freud, and Breton's response, after the exchange, shows in both writers an intense prickliness at work and in opposition. Both gentlemen protest a great deal, with both prides very much at stake. The entire controversy in a textually appended tea-pot, as it were, stirs up the issues of origination and self-analysis doubly. The tone of each correspondent speaks loudly indeed.

Freud's three letters, turning around the issue of Breton's having re-proached him for not including the name of Volkelt, an earlier writer on the symbolics of dream, within his bibliography, are a case study in the style of rumination, done on a great scale, by a master.

The very tone of the letters is striking, from the beginning, and Breton is finally right to perceive them as playing out a sort of quiet revenge (*coup sur coup*) – already in the first letter, Breton is to rest assured that Freud will read him, will read his "little book" that he hasn't yet gone very far in. The book may be little, although its resonance is great, to this day, but this seems a rather severe way of putting someone in his place. Now the name, begins Freud, *is* found there, along with that of Scherner, whose book on the symbolics of dream (1861) precedes that of Volkelt of 1878: "I am entitled therefore to ask you for an explanation." But the next para-graph does a switch: "To justify you, I now find that Volkelt's name is, in fact, not found in the bibliography of the French translation" (p. 201). Here begins the tale of justification.

A few hours later, Freud is back: "Excuse me if I return again to the Volkelt affair." It may not mean much to Breton, he continues, but he is very sensitive to such a reproach: "And when it comes from André Breton it is all the more painful for me" (p. 201). Freud writes that Volkelt's name was mentioned in the German edition but omitted in the French edition, "which justifies me and in some measure justifies you as well, although you could have been more prudent in the explanation of that state of things" (p. 202). Was Breton asking for justification? The whole trial seems a bit heavy.

Actually, the French translator Meyerson wasn't guilty either, because the name was omitted after the third printing of the German edition. (Still, we are reading what many of us might think of as an obsession on Freud's part about this justification Breton is supposed to have wanted to have.) On travels the blame, now to Otto Rank, who then took over the bibliography and is thus responsible for the omission, however unwit-ting, says Freud.

Then Freud's third letter, thanking Breton for answering him in detail (you could have been "briefer, just saying 'tant de bruit'" [p. 201]), reads like yet more blame, and certainly a little rejection; but then Breton, author, we remember, of a "little book" in the eyes of Freud, was kind enough to be considerate of what Freud calls "my special susceptibility on this point, probably a form of reaction against the excessive ambition of my childhood, luckily surmounted" (p. 203). Thus diagnosed, his rumination/obsession is explained, if not away, then at least into the daylight.

Freud ends by wondering exactly what the Surrealists (since they have manifested such an interest in *his* work) are up to. Now we can scarcely help noting the resemblance of Freud's seemingly peevish interrogation of the surrealist leader: "What does Surrealism want?" to the celebrated question phrased not so differently by the same master of psychoanalytic questioning: "What does woman want?" Indeed, to this question of Surrealism, Breton's answer could be supposed to have (already) been the manifestoes, the essays, but in particular this theory of communicating vessels. Freud read at least the first few pages of *Les Vases communicants,* but does not understand exactly what Surrealism intends, wants, means: "Perhaps after all I am not suited to understand it, I who am so far removed from art" (p. 204). Removing himself in this way – whether or not he considered himself so – from the world of "art" condemns Surrealism to be just there, in the world of art. Whereas Breton would have presumed it to be, would have demanded it to be, in the world as world. Precisely there is the issue, again, of justification, and thus an unavoidable one.

Quoting Freud in his reply to the effect that any forgetfulness is "motivated by a disagreeable feeling" (p. 205), Breton finds the whole thing symptomatic, particularly given the state of agitation manifested by the master. His further reflection on the difference between Freud's analysis of his own dreams and those he does of others leads him to the caustic comment which sums up his entire impression of the incident: "It still seems to me that in such a domain the fear of exhibitionism is not a sufficient excuse, and that in the search for objective truth, certain sacrifices are in order" (p. 206).

Here ends the odd exchange that concludes the volume on such a quirky note, and the praise of Freud's special *sensitivity,* as an homage rendered by one dream-obsessed writer to another, seems somehow to justify it within the realm of feeling, as within the realm of thought.

Pickles to Strawberries: Breton and the Others

In no other work of Breton, I think it safe to say, does the issue of the self and the other arise with such frequency, such force, and such problematic self-questioning, as in *Les Vases communicants.* That stands, to some extent, to reason, given the presiding metaphor and the overarching concern for the joining of one element and another, in the personal and in the conceptual dimensions.

Of course, the dreaming self is other to the thinking self, the emotional self to the rational self, the writing self to the living self. But the specifically bothersome issue that I want to take up occurs precisely in the space of a few pages at the very center of – at the very heart of – this all-important work.

The pages I am referring to are pages 102–14 in the 1955 printing, and they deal with the narrator's encounter of a young girl in front of a poster called *Pêché de Juive* (that title left somehow in suspense and not reflected upon), about whom he surmises a poverty (essential to him in his attraction to the opposite sex at this time, he says), and who reminds him first of a line from the loveliest poem of Charles Cros called "Liberty" ("Amie éclatante et brune"), a description he finds "insufficient and marvelous," and then, because of her eyes, of Gustave Moreau's watercolor called *Delilah*. After these three references to the world of "culture" – one perceived as a poster about blame, as it were, and two remembered, one with its words blamed for their insufficiency, as they fall short, and the other concerning the blameworthy Delilah with a power for seizure and desire – he then leaves the world of blame for the natural one. Here the feeling is of imminence rather than blame, and he speaks again of her eyes, but in their impression only, that of a drop of storm-cloud-sky-colored water falling on a body of calmer water and just touching it. This extensive description, continuing through the black shades first of India ink, then of an unutterable drabness in her clothing, before arriving at the sight of the perfect calf of her leg, reveals her as the source of further reflection; for she is in the vicinity of what Breton takes for the hospital Lariboisière, the maternity part. Thus, "the recognition of the marvelous *mother* potential in this young woman," and the linking of that to – the communicating of that with – his own desire to survive himself, is itself the source of the text. Blameless, in its origin.

The marvelous quality of the chanced-upon reflection on *origin,* giving birth to the text, brings to a head the continuing *émerveillement,* which climaxes in an extraordinary quest motif upon which she invites him – as damsel and wandering knight – to a charcuterie for some (above all things) pickles. Pickles, for she and her mother only enjoy meals accompanied by pickles. And this ordinary extraordinary detail somehow manages to reconnect the narrator with "everyday life" by an impossible-to-predict link, not totally devoid of lyricism:

Je me revois devant la charcuterie, reconcilié tout à coup par impossible avec la vie de tous les jours. Bien sûr, il est bon, il est supérieurement agréable de manger, avec quelqu'un qui ne vous soit pas tout à fait indifférent, des cornichons, par exemple. Il fallait bien que ce mot fût ici prononcé. La vie est faite aussi de ces petits usages, elle est fonction de ces goûts minimes qu'on a, qu'on n'a pas. Ces cornichons m'ont tenu lieu de providence, un certain jour. (p. 106)

(I see myself now in front of the store, suddenly reconciled – as if impossibly – with everyday life. Of course it is good, it is wonderfully delightful to eat, with someone who isn't completely indifferent to you, some pickles, for example. This word had to be pronounced here. Life is also made of these little customs, is also a function of these minimal tastes that you have, or don't. These pickles were my stand-in for providence, one day.)

The naturalists (apart from their pessimism) were the only ones who knew how to deal with situations of that sort, the narrator reflects, and they were, for that reason, far more poetic than the symbolists, for instance. And this very poetry of the everyday, for him, sets the girl in just the situation *Nadja* was set in, on another street, in another work, with another fate. Life takes on meaning for him, again, as it had then, with her, and the idealization of which he is more than conscious then sets in for him, followed, of course, by the letdown which occurs even within the surrealist marvelous.

Some of the saddest words of all time appear here, hidden deceptively in the middle of a paragraph: "Now that I am looking for her no longer, I meet her sometimes. Her eyes are still just as lovely, but it must be recognized that for me she has lost her charm" (p. 111). Her eyes of the fifth and the twelfth of April were visible again, but the image of the female face tended to hold less value with them.

Occupied entirely by his solitude, he then walks on the banks of the Marne river, envying the weekday workers now resting on the grass, in easy couple-harmony. "Two by two they had chosen each other, one day, . . ." and had no regrets; occupied by office details or a walk or a movie, or some children, they were participators in "regular life," in its not particularly productive solidity, which didn't have to be discussed or examined: it remained unquestioned. And this solid resistance, unquestioning and unchallenging, is what makes up life, leading, like the preceding passage up to the pickle-summit, to its own plaintive exclamation with its implicit wonder: "C'est tout de même pour ces gens qu'il y a des fraises dans les bois!" (p. 113). For them, nevertheless, these strawberries in the woods, and that too, unquestionably true.

For me, continues Breton, what is the reason for everything? Were I a great philosopher, poet, lover, revolutionary, there would be some excuse for the room I take up, but as it is, "comment justifier de la place qu'on occupe devant le manger, le boire, le revetir, le dormir?" (p. 114). Those who work deserve the room they take up; what do I deserve, exactly?

It is as if the pickles – that detail that gave its truth to the encounter with the sixteen-year-old who, finally, shared nothing in common with the narrator – as if they had met their match in the strawberries, giving their own truth to the Sunday outing from which the narrator is to be forever shut out. Neither pickles nor strawberries can be the detail that gives conviction to the writing-living life as he has lived it, and would live it through others. For they are always for someone else.

How indeed to justify the room taken up by any of us? That the passage should contain in its midst the strong reference to mothering and engendering is not without importance here – for is it not this very question of *justification* that gives its point (its lyric, problematic point) to Breton's moral concern? If not, how can we justify his dwelling on justification?

He is never in an equal match with these female wanderers in his volumes, those who drift along, through, and on. But each leaves a trace, even in his eventual boredom ("Nadja held no more interest for me"), disappointment ("the female image tended . . . to have less value"), and surface forgetting ("I had, in fact, forgotten everything of her profile . . ."). Like so many incarnations of the passerby, these figures will be lost, idealized for a moment, and then no longer recognized, among the pickles and the strawberries finally as unavailable as they are.

Is it that wandering through the streets or elsewhere has to be earned, imitated, written through? Among all the ironies of this most complicated dream book, that of the male/female problematic working itself out through the detail of absorption, admiration, and refusal is the most available. For Breton is always outside in these texts, watching – toward the final image of the muse shaking out her golden hair at the window – when everyone is already outside, carrying out the poetic operation in full daylight. In that daylight, someday, details may be shareable, the common ones and those of luxury, from pickles to strawberries, when the social question is settled, and the other finds his, and our, place. If there is, as Breton says of today, "little room for the one who would, haughtily, trace the knowing arabesque of suns" (p. 113), there is, on the contrary, room for the one-only-*among*-the-others: "This cloud has to draw its shadow over the page I am writing on, letting this tribute be paid to the plurality in which, in order to dare to write, I have to lose and find myself" (p. 184). The world of art, from which Freud claimed to be so removed, cannot suffice for Breton's project, and he must therefore find another presence.

That passage of losing and finding could stand as emblematic of the whole enterprise of these vessels communicating across the space of a great solitude, which it is the effort of the volume to transcend, and of the reader to grasp. That is, perhaps, the way in which the place we take up, in the world and not just the world of art, can be – at least for the moment of reading – *justified*.

Notes

1. André Breton, *Les Vases communicants* (Paris: Gallimard, 1933), 187 and 188. This work will appear in an English translation by Mary Ann Caws as *The Communicating Vessels* (Lincoln, Nebraska: University of Nebraska Press, 1988). All further references are to the Gallimard edition of 1955.

2. The reference is, of course, to Freud's question, taken up at the end of the essay.

Mysteries of Paris:
The Collective Uncanny in
André Breton's *L'Amour fou*

Margaret Cohen

André Breton's narratives are filled with uncanny happenings, "the most remarkable coincidences of desire and fulfillment, the most mysterious recurrences of similar experiences, in a particular place or on a particular date, the most deceptive sights and suspicious noises," as Sigmund Freud describes such events.[1] If uncanny manifestations for Freud proceed "from something familiar which has been repressed," Breton gives to this something familiar a content beyond individual experience.[2] Writing of the attraction exerted by various privileged Parisian structures in "Pont-Neuf," Breton states that their interest proceeds "pour une grande part de *ce qui a eu lieu* ici ou là et que, si nous tentions d'y voir clair, elles nous rendraient plus conscients de ce qui nous fait chanceler aussi bien que de ce qui nous rend l'équilibre" ["to a large extent from *what has taken place* here or there, and that, if we tried to clarify the matter, they would make us more conscious of what makes us unsteady as well as what gives us back our balance"].[3] Breton points here to the uncanny effect of the Parisian past on the present observer, implying, consonant with the Freudian understanding of the uncanny, the repressed relation of this past to the present. The following pages investigate how charged collective material haunts not only Breton's theory but also his practice. Using Freudian procedure to analyze the content of the uncanny experiences narrated by *L'Amour fou*'s "nuit du tournesol" ["night of the sunflower"], I will demonstrate the importance for Breton of an unstated social past.

Before turning to the night of the sunflower, it is useful to remember how the collective uncanny advanced by "Pont-Neuf" deviates from its Freudian inspiration. In suggesting collective experience as the source of uncanny material, Breton does not so much contradict Freud as dwell in the outer margins of Freud's theory, from which Freud prefers to retreat. Freud's essay on the uncanny proposes both an individual and a collective explanation for uncanny phenomena. Freud writes:

An uncanny experience occurs either when repressed infantile complexes have been revived by some impression, or when the primitive beliefs we have surmounted seem once more to be confirmed. Finally, we must not let our predilection for smooth solution and lucid exposition blind us to the fact that these two classes of uncanny experience are not always sharply distinguishable.[4]

While Freud goes on to subordinate the second class of uncanny experience to psychical existence, pointing out that primitive beliefs themselves recall the experiences of early childhood, Breton gives to previous collective beliefs a life of their own. Breton explicitly situates his socialized unconscious within the parameters of Freud's thought in *Les Vases communicants*, grounding this concept in a passage from *The Interpretation of Dreams:*

Freud, pour qui toute la substance du rêve est pourtant prise dans la vie réelle, ne résiste pas à la tentation de déclarer que "la nature intime de l'inconscient (essentielle réalité du psychique) nous est aussi inconnue que la réalité du monde extérieur," donnant ainsi des gages à ceux-là mêmes que sa méthode avait le mieux failli mettre en déroute.[5]

[Freud, for whom the entire substance of the dream is, however, taken from real life, cannot resist stating that "the intimate nature of the unconscious (essential psychical reality) is as unknown to us as the reality of the exterior world," giving thus tokens to those whom his method had almost best put to flight.]

Just how Freud gives "tokens to those whom his method had almost best put to flight" emerges in Breton's dizzying experience on the night of the sunflower.[6] Among the multiple uncanny moments narrated by Breton's promenade, perhaps the most uncanny occurs in the area surrounding the Tour Saint-Jacques. If "Tournesol" describes this structure with a term used by "Pont-Neuf" to explain the uncanny effect of *"what has taken place"* – "A Paris la Tour Saint-Jacques *chancelante* / Pareille à un tournesol" – the text of "la nuit du tournesol" situates the structure within a historical context.[7] Breton mentions

des circonstances assez troubles qui ont présidé à son édification et auxquelles on sait que le rêve millénaire de la transmutation des métaux est étroitement lié. Il n'est pas jusqu'au virement du bleu au rouge en quoi réside la propriété spécifique du tournesol-réactif dont le rappel ne soit sans doute justifié par analogie avec les couleurs distinctives de Paris, dont, au reste, ce quartier de la Cité est le berceau, de Paris qu'exprime ici d'une façon tout particulièrement organique, *essentielle,* son Hôtel de Ville que nous laissons sur notre gauche en nous dirigeant vers le Quartier Latin. Je cède à l'adorable vertige auquel m'inclinent peut-être ces lieux où tout ce que j'aurai le mieux connu a commencé (70–71, Breton's emphasis).

[the rather disturbed circumstances which presided over its construction, and to which it is known that the thousand-year-old dream of the transmutation of metals is closely linked. Even a recall of the change from blue to red which constitutes the specific property of litmus paper [literally: reactive-sunflower] can doubtless be justified by analogy with the distinctive colors of Paris, for which, moreover, this quarter of the city is the cradle, of Paris which is expressed here in a particularly organic and essential way by its Hôtel de Ville, which we leave on our left in heading towards the Latin Quarter. I give way to the adorable dizziness to which, perhaps, I am inclined by these scenes where everything that I will have best known began.]

Much has been written on the importance of alchemy for Breton's project, and I neglect it here not only because of such prior discussion but also because the alchemical past, mentioned in the opening sentence above, is hardly repressed within Breton's own text. Breton alludes vaguely to other Parisian pasts, however, when he calls the "quartier de la Cité" "the cradle of Paris," and he dwells particularly on the Hôtel de Ville, for him an organic and essential expression of Paris.

If the past which he invokes is obscure for a reader distanced in time and space, it was less so for Breton's contemporaries. Descriptive writings on the city of Paris from the 1920s and 1930s consistently associate the Hôtel de Ville with the past of Parisian revolution. According to the *Guide Bleu:*

Among the events which the Hôtel de Ville witnessed before the Revolution, we will mention the uprising of the Maillotins in 1358, the first festivals which were held there in 1606, at the entrance of Henry IV into the capital, the troubles of the Fronde. But the importance of this structure dates above all from 1789. The three hundred electors named by the districts of Paris made it the site of their reunions. July 17, 1789, Louis XVI received there from the hands of Bailly, mayor of Paris, the tricolored cockade. In 1792, the 172 committee members designated by the sections of Paris and installed in their turn in the Hôtel de Ville gave there the signal for the insurrection of August 10. On 9 Thermidor, year II (July 27, 1794), Robespierre, who had found shelter there with his friends, was arrested to be taken to the scaffold.[8]

The *Guide* goes on, after a break for several royal christenings and weddings, to narrate the defense of the Hôtel de Ville in 1830 by the Swiss guards of the king, its importance in the revolutions of 1848 and 1871 as the site from which the 1848 Republic and 1871 Commune were proclaimed, and its subsequent burning by the Commune. Charles Fegdal gives a more enthusiastic narration of the nineteenth-century memories associated with this spot in the twentieth century: "From the month of February to the month of June 1848, the life of Lamartine is that of all Paris, the life of France itself. The Hôtel-de-Ville will be the soul of this tumultuous, rapid, and magnificent life. At the Hôtel-de-Ville, at the side of Lamartine, we are going to witness a series of desperate and heroic struggles for the triumph of republican ideas."[9]

While Breton does not mention a revolutionary past when he wanders through the cradle of Paris on the night of the sunflower, such a past is not entirely absent from *L'Amour fou*'s fourth chapter, displaced from Breton's narrative of his experience to his commentary on the poem. Linking each line in "Tournesol" with an episode from "la nuit du tournesol," Breton allies "Le bal des innocents battait son plein / Les lampions prenaient feu lentement dans les marronniers" with "le berceau de Paris" (80). He explains that the "bal des innocents" recalls the former *charnier des innocents* at the Tour Saint-Jacques, mentioning also alchemical historical details associated with this *Tour*. He then glosses the revolutionary resonances of "lampions" by referring to the nickname of his companion: "le directeur de l'établissement l'avait un jour appelée publiquement Quatorze Juillet" [the director of the place had one day called her publicly the Fourteenth of July] (87). Given Breton's immediately prior demonstration of familiarity with the details of Parisian history, it is curious that he does not cite instances from the Parisian cradle's rich revolutionary past. Perhaps Breton displaces revolution from the streets of Paris to the music hall to trivialize political struggle. Displacement is, however, also a mechanism familiar from Freudian descriptions of repression, suggesting that revolutionary ghosts in this text may be subject to a Freudian model of historical relation.

Oblique allusions in Breton's vertiginous experience of the "quartier de la Cité" confirm his Freudian understanding of the relation between revolutionary past and present. When Breton calls the area "le berceau de Paris," he evokes the specific textual past of Victor Hugo's *Notre-Dame de Paris*. Giving literary currency to a commonplace from descriptive writings on Paris, Hugo states in the chapter "Paris à vol d'oiseau," "Paris est né, comme on sait, dans cette vieille île de la Cité qui a la forme d'un berceau" ["Paris was born, as is known, in this old île de la Cité which has the shape of a cradle"].[10] If Hugo and the guidebook writers apply this figure to the Ile de la Cité, not only shaped like a cradle but also the original Paris, Breton displaces the cradle of Paris to include an area not part of the original Lutetia, the right bank near the Seine. He thus implies that the founding Parisian status of this second area's unmentioned past, as revolution, conforming to a Freudian description of repressed material, holds great value for the subject repressing. A second Hugo allusion in the passage quoted above supports a Freudian understanding of the relation between present and past, for it links the "quartier de la Cité" not only to Paris past, but to a Paris whose past has been effaced. When Breton terms the Tour Saint-Jacques "le grand monument du monde à l'irrévélé" ["the world's great monument to the unrevealed"], he recalls Hugo's comments on the Tour in "Paris à vol d'oiseaux" (69). Hugo writes: "Il lui manquait en particulier ces quatre monstres qui, aujourd'hui encore, perchés aux encoignures de son toit, ont l'air de quatre sphinx qui donnent à deviner au nouveau Paris l'énigme de l'ancien" ["It lacked, in particular, these four monsters which, today still, perched on the corners of its roof, seem like four sphinxes which pose to the new Paris the riddle of the old"], formulating in pre-Freudian terms the power of repressed Parisian ghosts to insist in the present.[11]

If Breton's uncanny responds to elided revolutionary material, this material should be both repressed by Breton and familiar to him, for the

Freudian uncanny, we remember, comes from "something familiar which has been repressed." In Freudian explanations of persisting repressed material, the past material, generally both unpleasant and attractive, continues to trouble the subject, imperfectly integrated into his current conscious life. Revolution holds such an ambiguous position in Breton's own project, although it belongs to a more recent past than the repressed childhood material discussed by orthodox Freudianism. Concrete revolutionary activity is one of the great concerns of Surrealism in the 1920s, and throughout Breton's writings from this period he makes demands for the street uprisings characteristic of nineteenth-century Parisian revolutions. Breton's relation to practical revolution is troubled, however, by his experience with the French Communist Party in the late twenties and early thirties. By the time that he writes *L'Amour fou,* he has distanced himself from practical revolution, largely replacing the word "révolution" in his text with the ambiguous "jusqu'à un nouvel ordre." While Breton elides not only a mention of revolution but also its historical presence in the spots which he visits, it insists, as we have seen, in repressed form, an "unlaid ghost," as Freud calls such material, for Breton's disillusion with concrete revolution in no way dilutes his critique of the existing social order.[12]

Collective forces also encourage Breton's repression of a revolutionary past in the cradle of Paris. The "quartier de la Cité" was among the spaces most profoundly modified by the Baron Haussmann's post-1848 reconstruction of Paris. This reconstruction had multiple goals, for Haussmann sought to stimulate the Parisian economy, facilitate circulation, improve public health, and beautify the city, but it also had an undeniable strategic motive which Anthony Sutcliffe describes as follows:

Ever since 1789 no Government had been safe from the threat of violent overthrow in the streets of Paris. The traditional tactics of revolutionaries were to take over the centre and east of the city and seize the Hôtel de Ville, where a free commune could be proclaimed and money and printing presses were available. Barricades had been erected in Paris nine times in the twenty-five years before the Second Empire, and a small number of amateurs could use them in the narrow streets to hold off large numbers of troops, at least for a time. If broad thoroughfares could be driven through these turbulent districts, troops would be able to penetrate quickly to the source of any trouble. They would be too wide to be blocked by barricades (or so it was thought).[13]

Such a program targeted the area around the Hôtel de Ville. A strategic site requiring immediate military accessibility, this *quartier* was also at the center of a working-class population who, in the previous sixty-five years, had provided the impetus to revolutionary activity.

The Hôtel de Ville, Breton's "organique, *essentielle*" expression of Paris, is associated with the Parisian past of revolution and repression in multiple ways. Not only the center of revolutionary activity, it is also the administrative center responsible for the reconstruction of central Paris. In addition, it is itself a product of such repressive reconstruction. No "organique" part of the cradle of Paris, the Hôtel de Ville was rebuilt in the 1870s following its destruction by the Paris Commune, and Breton draws attention to its artificial nature with the trope of reversal familiar to Freud's patients. Like its surroundings, however, the Hôtel de Ville pretends to old age, concealing the disturbances which led to its reconstruction. It thus serves in the social realm a function similar to Freud's screen memory in the psychical realm, "not the genuine memory-trace but a later revision of it, a revision which may have been subjected to the influences of a variety of later psychical forces."[14] If Breton seeks in L'Amour fou "to reconcile . . . Engels and Freud" the collective mechanisms of repression at work in the cradle of Paris indicate one point of reconciliation (31). These mechanisms result from the bourgeoisie's effort to efface the proletarian forces threatening its hegemony, as they illustrate Marx and Engels's explanation of historical process as class struggle. In a situation of class struggle, Freudian techniques of reading become applicable to collective history, for such techniques provide a way to locate the persistence of a subversive and obscured past in the seemingly coherent constructions of the ruling ideology.

A second Parisian past lurks on the night of the sunflower, appearing, like the revolutionary past, in the disfigured and oblique manner which characterizes Freudian repressed material. On the track of latent content, Freud juxtaposes seemingly unrelated moments within the patient's discourse, sparking hidden similarities. A similar juxtaposition of the spots visited by Breton reveals an effaced bohemian Paris past. Moving from the Café des Oiseaux in Montmartre to the Ile de la Cité, Breton juxtaposes the present center of Parisian prostitution to its center one hundred years before.[15] Appropriately, "les petites rues du quartier des Halles" occupy an intermediate moment in Breton's movement. Both a present and a past site of prostitution, these streets provide spatial and temporal links between Montmartre and the "quartier de la Cité." The seedy past sparked by Breton's route through Paris is familiar to any reader of Eugène Sue's Les Mystères de Paris, and Breton's promenade alludes in characteristically oblique manner to Sue's novel, explicitly discussed in Les Vases communicants. His route from the right bank to the Ile de la Cité retraces the steps which open the Mystères and leads him to the Marché aux Fleurs dear to Sue's heroine, Fleur-de-Marie, where he compares his own companion to a flower. A reminder of the Parisian cradle's bohemian past also lurks in Breton's allusion to Hugo discussed above, for Notre-Dame de Paris calls up an even more distant central Paris of pleasure and crime.

To determine why the past of prostitution haunts Breton's uncanny experience of the Parisian cradle, we could point, as with a revolutionary past, to collective reasons at work in this past's effacement. The class struggle which exiled the workers from central Paris resulted also in a marginalization of Parisian prostitution. Such simultaneous marginalization was not coincidental. Prostitutes in the nineteenth century were often confused by the bourgeoisie with revolutionaries, considered the consorts of revolutionary men, and, like them, a threat to the morality of bourgeois society.[16]

If the cradle of Paris is haunted by the bourgeoisie's nineteenth-century marginalization of prostitution, Breton alludes elsewhere in *L'Amour fou* to a text positing the responsibility of bourgeois society for the prostitution which it condemns. In the fifth chapter of *L'Amour fou*, Breton quotes from Engels's discussion of prostitution in *The Origin of the Family*. According to Engels, bourgeois society both maintains the existence of a proletarian class whose women, out of necessity, turn to prostitution, and relegates bourgeois women to the position of proletarians within the bourgeoisie, transforming all sexual commerce between men and women into an economic relation. For Engels, monogamous sexual love between men and women will only come to fruition with the abolition of private property, and it is this moment from Engels's argument which appears in Breton's text. Breton asserts that "la propriété privée une fois abolie, 'on peut affirmer avec raison,' déclare Engels, 'que *loin de disparaître, la monogamie sera plutôt pour la première fois réalisée'*" ["once private property has been abolished, 'we can reasonably affirm,' declares Engels, 'that *far from disappearing, monogamy will rather be realized for the first time'*] (112). He does not, however, cite the remainder of Engels's paragraph, which runs as follows: "For with the transformation of the means of production into social property there will disappear also wage labor, the proletariat, and therefore the necessity for a certain – statistically calculable – number of women to surrender themselves for money. Prostitution disappears; monogamy, instead of collapsing, at least becomes a reality – also for men."[17] Eliding the bourgeois relation to prostitution not only at the site of its historical effacement but also in a text where it is unavoidably present, Breton leads us to ask if reasons other than the historical displacement of prostitution may dictate its repression in *L'Amour fou*.

Breton's visits to current sites of Parisian prostitution on the night of the sunflower heightens our suspicion that his text represses prostitution's present as well as its past. When he visits Montmartre and Les Halles, he names places known at the time as prostitutes' hangouts but refuses to describe their ambiance, using the oblique allusion found in Freudian texts of repression. He mentions the Montmartre Café des Oiseaux, known in 1934 as a meeting-place for the "bourgeoise en goguette" ["bourgeoisie out for a good time"] and the "peuple de la nuit," the prostitutes and cocaine dealers who catered to their needs.[18] He also names a "petit torchon renommé" ["well-known joint"] of Les Halles, the Chien qui fume, as the adjective "renommé" raises the issue of the restaurant's reputation which it, however, fails to specify (68). Parisian guides of the time supplement Breton's lacuna:

Thus, on leaving the *Grappe d'Or,* take the *rue des Halles,* already beginning to wake up, to go and eat oysters or onion-soup at the *Restaurant du Chien qui fume,* rue du Pont-Neuf, corner of rue Berger.
At three in the morning, the ground-floor, the small saloons on the first floor, and private rooms are all full of supper.
The very motley ensemble is most interesting. The lady in evening-dress is side by side with the young workgirl or the hatless prostitute.[19]

Lurking in Breton's mention of both locales is the interface between bourgeois and prostitute, a content also implicit in the other aspects of repressed prostitution mentioned, as Engels describes the bourgeoisie's responsibility for the institution which it condemns, and the cradle of Paris hides the bourgeoisie's exiling of prostitution from central Paris. I could use collective issues to explain why the relation between bourgeoisie and prostitute is repeatedly repressed throughout *L'Amour fou,* for the various scenes of class interface implicit in Breton's text raise, in differing fashions, the bourgeoisie's repressive attitude towards sexuality attacked by Breton through his writings. Such an explanation would, however, open up historical and psychoanalytic issues beyond the scope of this current essay. Instead, I want to conclude by reflecting on the personal reasons dictating the repressed presence of bourgeois-prostitute relations on the night of the sunflower.

I suggested that Breton repressed a mention of revolution because it raised for him an unresolved surrealist problem, the reconciliation of surrealist poetic practice with practical revolutionary activity. The relation of prostitute to bourgeois points towards another, and related, Bretonian antinomy, if we understand it as the relation of prostitute to bourgeois surrealist poet. Prostitutes hold for Breton an ambiguous position. They are victims of the bourgeois society which he challenges, but they also provide a model for the surrealist *flâneur.* Like the surrealist stroller, they live contiguously, available to the unknown, to chance events and to passers-by, and in *Nadja,* Breton invokes a prose poem by Baudelaire, "Les Foules" ["The Crowds"], which explicitly asserts prostitution as a metaphor for poetic activity. Prostitution also, however, indicates the limit of Breton's social critique, for in his dealings with non-metaphorical prostitutes, Breton displays attitudes allying him with the bourgeoisie which he attacks. While interested in Nadja, Breton never falls in love with her, and, repelled by the sordid details of her life, eventually judges her with the morally weighted "tomber": "celle qui *tombait,* parfois" ["she who sometimes fell"].[20] In *Les Vases communicants,* Breton asserts, "Il ne m'est *jamais* arrivé de coucher avec une prostituée, ce qui tient, d'une part, à ce que je n'ai jamais aimé – et à ce que je ne crois pas pouvoir aimer – une prostituée" ["To sleep with a prostitute is something that has never happened to me, which has to do partly with the fact that I have never loved – and that I do not think myself capable of loving – a prostitute"], as the profession of prostitution irrevocably diminishes a woman for him.[21]

It remains, of course, to speculate more extensively on the motives dictating the repression which the preceding pages have described. Does Breton strategically obscure prostitution and proletarian revolution, reproducing these issues' repressed status within bourgeois society in order to call the reader's attention precisely to this repressed status, or do such issues inadvertently haunt his discourse? Is repression a literary device used by an author most familiar with Freud's theories to express the social contradictions in which he sees himself caught, or does such repression proceed from more profound unconscious motivations? It is certainly tempting to use psychoanalytic conclusions to explain Breton's repression of prostitution, since this repression recalls Freud's statement that "neurotic males declare that they feel there is something uncanny about the female genital organs. This *unheimlich* place, however, is the former *heim* [home] of all human beings."[22] Such an explanation would be most convincing if it took account of the challenge posed by Breton to Freudian method. Conceiving the subject as the intersection of interior and exterior forces, Breton's collective uncanny provides another example of his interest in reconciling Marxist and Freudian theory. In order to construct the link between *L'Amour fou*'s textual and biographical subject, the reader needs first to rethink the relation of transhistorical psychoanalytic categories to historicized social experience.

Notes

1. Sigmund Freud, "The 'Uncanny'" [*Das 'Unheimliche'*] (1919), in *The Standard Edition of the Complete Psychological Works of Sigmund Freud*, ed. James Strachey (London: Hogarth Press, 1953–74), 17, 248.

2. Ibid., 247.

3. André Breton, "Pont-Neuf," in *La Clé des champs* (Paris: Editions du Sagittaire, 1953), 229–30, Breton's emphasis.

4. Freud, "The 'Uncanny,'" 249.

5. André Breton, *Les Vases communicants* (Paris: Gallimard, 1981), 18.

6. Ibid.

7. André Breton, *L'Amour fou* (Paris: Gallimard, 1982), 70, my emphasis. Page numbers within the text of the paper refer to this edition.

8. *Les Guides bleus: Paris et ses environs* (Paris: Hachette, 1924), 169.

9. Charles Fegdal, *La Fleur des curiosités de Paris* (Paris: Editions de la Revue Contemporaine, 1921), 207.

10. Victor Hugo, *Notre-Dame de Paris* (Paris: Garnier-Flammarion, 1967), 139.

11. Ibid., 152.

12. Sigmund Freud, "Analysis of a Phobia in a Five-Year-Old Boy" [*Analyse der Phobie eines fünfjährigen Knaben*] (1909), in *The Standard Edition*, 10, 122.

13. Anthony Sutcliffe, *The Autumn of Central Paris* (London: Edward Arnold, 1970), 31.

14. Sigmund Freud, *The Psychopathology of Everyday Life* [*Zur Psychopathologie des Alltagslebens*] (1901) in *The Standard Edition*, 6, 148.

15. For a discussion of the history of Montmartre, see Louis Chevalier's *Montmartre du plaisir et du crime* (Paris: Robert Laffont, 1980).

16. For a discussion of bourgeois attitudes towards prostitution, see Jill Harsin, *Policing Prostitution in Nineteenth-Century France* (Princeton, New Jersey: Princeton University Press, 1985).

17. Frederick Engels, *The Origin of the Family, Private Property and the State* (New York: International Publishers, 1972), 139.

18. Chevalier, *Montmartre du plaisir et du crime*, 370.

19. *Pleasure Guide to Paris* (Paris: Management, 1927), 129.

20. André Breton, *Nadja* (Paris: Gallimard, 1977), 134.

21. Breton, *Les Vases communicants*, 84.

22. Freud, "The 'Uncanny,'" 248.

The Communicating Labyrinth: Breton's "La Maison d'Yves" as a Micro-*Manifeste*

John Zuern

> La peinture, la poésie, chacune dans son domaine propre, devaient nécessairement s'appliquer un jour à retrouver le chemin qui mène aux Mères, à la plus profonde des profondeurs.
>
> Andre Breton[1]

André Breton's "La Maison d'Yves,"[2] in which Breton pays tribute to Yves Tanguy, presents itself as an inviting venue for the exploration of the surrealist aesthetic both in literature and the visual arts. The poem's interest lies not only in its testimony to Breton's enthusiastic support of the work of fellow avant-garde artists, but a careful reading reveals that in "La Maison d'Yves" Breton's tribute to Tanguy develops into an expression of the fundamental principles of surrealist aesthetics. The structure of the "Maison" shows itself to be essentially labyrinthine. The form of the labyrinth has close affinities to the images Breton himself uses to describe the surrealist orientation to the world, in particular the "tissu capillaire"[3] which lies between the realms of the unconscious and external reality. The labyrinth has been observed as an organizational principle in a wide range of surrealist productions in the visual arts.[4] An examination of the grammar in "La Maison d'Yves" reveals that the poem, in spite of its title, is as much concerned with a process as with a static structure; the process it describes is precisely the activity of the surrealist artist. The association of images in the poem is closely linked to its labyrinthine structure, and particular images, namely the references to mythological heroes, expand the parameters of the poem so that it will admit a reading which takes into account Breton's conviction that the surrealist world view is not limited to aesthetics, but has profound social ramifications. These considerations support a view of "La Maison d'Yves" as a comprehensive statement – and formal emblem – of the surrealist vision.

One variety of the labyrinth[5] is a closed structure which contains within its parameters a number – ideally, an infinite number – of variables. In "La Maison d'Yves," the closure is provided by the inaugurating rhymed couplet, "La maison d'Yves Tanguy / Où l'on n'entre que la nuit," and the final line, "C'est la maison d'Yves Tanguy," which, in fusing with the initial line to form the sentence "La maison d'Yves Tanguy, c'est la maison d'Yves Tanguy," effectively seals the poem: the poem's maze unfolds in the copula of this sentence. The five rhymed couplets which follow the first at intervals throughout the poem can be seen as additional structural support. It is in the intervals between the couplets that the volatile, variable, and *potentially infinite* dimension of the poem develops the pattern, reminiscent of certain children's songs, of cumulative, repeating lines that do not rhyme and, at first, seem to bear no semantic relation to one another. The couplets, formally closed and finite, contain the essentially open and perpetual form of the cumulative pattern. Thus, the most superficial observation of the physical "building" of "La Maison d'Yves" reveals the poem's labyrinthine nature.

If we focus our attention on the images contained both in the couplets and in the accumulating lines, we can observe a relationship between the two forms that is more than structural and spatial. The couplets do not simply contain the cumulative lines, but determine their content. The image set forward in each of the seven couplets in the series exerts an influence on the images contained in the next line in the accruing series; the image that bears no apparent relation to its immediate neighbors harks back to the foregoing couplet. From the standpoint of the distribution of images in the poem, the couplets might be likened to bar magnets placed under a page in a classroom demonstration of the gravitational force: metal filings spread over the page arrange themselves in looping patterns, clustering at the poles of the magnet; in a similar manner, each new image that appears, seemingly at random, in the cumulative sequence loops upward along a line of thematic force to the affiliated image in the couplet above it. The images that build "La Maison d'Yves" arrange themselves along three very general lines of force: the first encompassing the ideas of entry, piercing, and seeking; the second the ideas of enclosure, restriction, and the confounding of external and internal space; the third the idea of a guiding line.

The relationship between the first couplet and the first line in what will become the cumulative sequence is not difficult to determine. The lines "La maison d'Yves Tanguy / Où l'on n'entre que la nuit / Avec la lampe tempête" comprise the ideas of entry, darkness, and the light with which one pierces the darkness. These lines prescribe the conditions under which one may enter the "house": night, of course, is associated with dreams, the unconscious, and the unknown – the domain of the surrealist artist which he seeks to bring into contact with the external world. The "lampe tempête" is a source of light in unusual, perhaps dangerous circumstances, and may indicate the Surrealist's supernormal vision, which is his guide as he enters the unknown and occasionally perilous realm of the unconscious and of dream.

The image of piercing vision is continued in the next couplet/line unit, "Dehors le pays transparent / Un devin dans son élément. . . . Avec la scierie si laborieuse qu'on ne la voit plus." The first line introduces the important opposition of inside and outside space. Here, the external appears to be clearly separate from the internal; the "pays" is "dehors." The image of the couplet is not difficult to understand; its first line calls to mind the limpid atmosphere of Tanguy's enigmatic landscapes, its second the frequent association of the surrealist artist with the seer, as well as the title of Breton's tribute to another of his contemporaries, *Picasso dans son élément.*[6] The "scierie" is more startling, but it can be seen as a radical combination of the ideas of the couplet — transparency and piercing. The sawmill reminds us, too, that a house is being built — as a sawmill supplies the lumber for actual houses, "the scierie" here supplies another image in the structure that becomes the house of Yves Tanguy.

The third couplet is puzzling in that its lines seem unrelated: "Et la toile de Jouy du ciel / Vous, chassez le surnaturel." These lines, however, begin the enfolding of images of space that render the poem a labyrinth, as well as introduce the mythical figures who people it. The union of the decorative fabric "toile du Jouy" with the sky confounds inner, furnished space with the "pays" outside. The "toile de Jouy" may also refer to the "toiles" of Tanguy, which almost always depict objects distributed in an indeterminate space. The "vous" who is commanded to "hunt the supernatural" emerges, upon a rereading of the poem, as Theseus, who, aided by Ariadne, solves the labyrinth and defeats the Minotaur. The imperative here serves to reinforce the foregoing idea of entry: Theseus (and the surrealist artist, and the reader) is compelled to enter the labyrinth which is at this point in the poem beginning to take shape. The line associated with this couplet, "Avec toutes les étoiles de sacrebleu," takes up the sky image of the "toile de Jouy" and, with its confounded stars from which one cannot get one's bearings, continues to construct the maze. At this point in the poem the cumulative sequence has taken shape, and generates its own sense of imperative: the insistence of the repetition drives the reader onward to the anticipated new image and thus deeper into the poem and the poem's maze.

The relationship between the images in the couplets and those in the cumulative lines was described above as a loop; in the fourth — and therefore the central — couplet, the loop itself appears as an image: "Elle est de lassos et de jambages / Couleur d'écrivesse à la nage." In combination with its companion line in the sequence, "Avec les tramways en tous sens ramenés à leur seules antennes," this central couplet describes the actual structure of the poem's linked images — for "elle," that is, "la maison d'Yves," indeed reveals itself to be of "lassos and curlicues" — as well as introduces the motif of the guiding line. The reference to the color of a swimming crayfish may relate to a particular painting's colors, but it would appear that the reference to a crayfish in motion contributes to the image of movement of – or is determined by – a line, whether a lasso, a written curl, the antennae of a crayfish or the guiding poles of the tramcar that attach it to its guiding wire. Connecting wires and antenna-like extensions can be found in many of Tanguy's paintings, particularly those which he produced around the time of this poem's composition, *Arrières pensées* (1939) and *Les Mouvements et les actes* (1937).[7] The verb *ramener*, with its sense of bringing back, recalling, may play a part in the image of restriction to a particular space which is overtly stated in the following couplet.

As in the third couplet, both the labyrinth and the mythological adventurers associated with quests for the supernatural are presented in the fifth couplet/line conjunction. "L'espace lié, le temps réduit" describes the labyrinthine structure. A labyrinth "binds" space in that it concentrates it in a limited area; the radii of the plane are bent and folded in on themselves. In a like manner, the linear progress of time is enfolded in the structure of the labyrinth.[8] Both "Ariane dans sa chambre étui" and "l'argonaute" of the line "Avec la crinière sans fin de l'argonaute" are figures involved in journeys ending in a confrontation with the surreal. The "crinière" picks up the image of the line, and here it is "endless," running through the infinite permutations of the labyrinth. The "chambre étui" in which we find Ariane is perplexing, for it seems to indicate that Ariane, rather than waiting outside the labyrinth as she does in the legend, is herself enclosed. The pattern of enclosing and enfolding may extend so far that that which proposes itself to be a guide through the maze is itself confounded in the maze. I will pick up this thread at a later point.

Interior and exterior space are confounded in the sixth couplet/line pair. The couplet, "Le service est fait par les sphinges / Qui se couvrent les yeux de linges," suggests, with its image of riddling attendants who cover their eyes with the linens, the interior space of the puzzling "house" the poem is constructing. This whimsical image gains a great deal of energy from the companion line in the accumulating sequence, "Avec le mobilier fulgurant du désert," which combines an image of great space, "désert," with a domestic image, "le mobilier." When brought together, the couplet and the line create an interconnected double image of the expanse of the Egyptian desert with the pyramids and the enigmatic sphinx and of a bizarrely furnished household maintained by servants whose only wish is to confound. Both of these physical spaces are contained in the maze that is the house of Yves Tanguy: "le mobilier fulgarant du désert," of course, refers to Tanguy's painted landscapes, in which strikingly clear – if puzzling – objects furnish an otherwise vacant and seemingly limitless plain.

In the final couplet the "on" of the first lines reappears: "On y meurtrit on y guérit / On y complote sans abri." This sudden description of activity effects an urgency, as does the "Vous, chassez le surnaturel" of the third couplet, and unites this "vous" with the impersonal pronoun of the first couplet. The actor here is Theseus, and Theseus is the surrealist artist who must confront the Minotaur of the unconscious, the unknown, the dreamt. That the Minotaur is a compelling figure to the surrealist imagination is testified to by the title of one of the movement's longest-running reviews, *Minotaure,* which appeared with covers on which leading surrealist artists depicted the beast.[9] The ambivalence with which Surrealism seems to regard its mascot is indicative of its recognition of the precariousness of the unconscious realm in which one can either achieve liberation or descend into madness.[10] The Minotaur is attractive but dangerous, potentially both creative and destructive, a wounding and a healing force. This dialectical approach to the unconscious may well be figured in the line "On y meurtrit on y guérit." If the verbs are taken as transitive, however, the line can be read as a formula for the surrealist method: the Surrealist's "plot" against the mundane external world, involving a kind of violence, a radical dissociation and reassociation of elements which then "heal" into a fresh vision.[11] This couplet is linked to the final line in the cumulative series, "Avec les signes qu'échangent de loin les amoureux," by means of the Theseus/Ariane theme. The words "de loin," the distance across which these lovers communicate, are particularly resonant, given the previous images of expanses in the poem – expanses which have been enfolded in the poem's labyrinth. As the last unit in a potentially infinite series, this line bears a great deal of weight. It consolidates the image of the labyrinth as an enfolded space – Theseus and Ariane are connected across its distance by the guiding line; it extends the human element of the poem to include "les amoureux," not only Theseus and Ariane but the poem's readers; and it returns us to Tanguy's paintings, in which indeterminate objects or beings stand at tremendous distances from one another but appear to "communicate," either along connecting lines or by means of unifying spatial relationships. Finally, the line closes the sequence with the idea of exchange, a dynamic activity that provides a clue to the function of this imaginary labyrinth.

"If Breton envisages himself as a Theseus forever closed within a labyrinth of crystal, at least he intends to confer upon the labyrinth a movement as perpetual as his within it," writes Mary Ann Caws in her biography of Breton.[12] And indeed, Breton's labyrinth in "La Maison d'Yves" is in motion. In fact, a consideration of the grammar of the first lines and of the cumulative sequence will show that the poem is essentially about an *activity.* Each accumulating line is predicated grammatically on the first couplet, "La maison d'Yves / Où l'on n'entre que la nuit," in that each, beginning with "avec," indicates something brought *into* "la maison d'Yves." The additive sequences refer to the mode of entry into the "house," although at the end of the poem the "house" is built of their images, with the couplets – with their own images and oblique references to structure – serving as a formal skeleton. Thus, one constructs "la maison d'Yves" in the very act of entering it. This feature of the poem, highly satisfying from a surrealist point of view, depends upon the repetition/accumulation line pattern reminiscent of children's songs such as the English "House that Jack Built" and the French "Petit Bricou," which relate a process made up of linked actions in sequence. Breton adopts this pattern, but fractures the sequence and creates a looping maze rather than a linear progression. Yet the urgent tempo of the pattern maintains the notion of activity and movement. "La Maison d'Yves" is ultimately a portrayal of surrealist liminality, of the process of creation and the artist's approach to the "pointe sublime" or the "point de l'esprit" at which oppositions "cessent d'être perçus contradictoirement."[13]

That the combinatory process of surrealist creation can be at least partially visualized with the image of a maze is evident in reading Breton's theoretical writings on Surrealism. In his discussions of the objectives of the movement, Breton himself often turns to images suggestive of labyrinthine structures. In *Les Vases communicants,* in which he attempts to lay the groundwork for a union of the external, physical realm with the realm of the unconscious and of dreams, he describes the unifying agent as a "tissu capillaire":

Le rôle de ce tissu est, on l'a vu, d'assurer l'échange constant qui doit se produire dans la pensée entre le monde extérieur et le monde intérieur, échange qui nécessite l'interpénétration continue de l'activité de veille et de l'activité de sommeil. Toute mon ambition a été de donner ici un aperçu de sa structure.[14]

Breton makes the statement, also in *Les Vases communicants:* "Je souhaite qu'il [le surréalisme] passe pour n'avoir tenté rien de mieux que de jeter un *fil conducteur* entre les mondes pas trop dissociés de la veille et du sommeil, de la réalité extérieure et intérieure, de la raison et de la folie, du calme de la connaissance et de l'amour, de la vie pour la vie et de la révolution, etc."[15] The "fil conducteur" can be read as a "conducting wire," participating in the imagery of electricity of which Breton was fond, or as a "conducting thread," suggesting a "fil d'Ariane" that traverses the space between the two opposing realms, a dynamic in the surrealist dialectic. If the "tissu capillaire," suggestive of a conduit composed of convoluted passages, and the "fil conducteur" indicate the structure of the surrealist orientation to the two opposing "worlds," Breton's references to "le vertige" describe the experiential, active dimension of this orientation.[16] The surrealist imagination must break down the accepted structures of the exterior world and reestablish them in new and unexpected combinations with elements from the interior world of the unconscious, and must always dismiss the actual in favor of the possible. The "ideal atmosphere," Breton writes in "L'Introduction sur le peu de réalité," ". . . would be one in which

116

what could exist destroys at every step what does exist."[17] In *Manifeste du surréalisme* (1924), Breton indicates that the imagination itself is labyrinthine in nature, and upholds the value of this quality:

La seule imagination me rend compte de ce qui *peut être*, et c'est assez pour lever un peu le terrible interdit; assez aussi pour que je m'abandonne à elle sans crainte de me tromper (comme si l'on pouvait se tromper davantage). Où commence-t-elle à devenir mauvaise et où s'arrête la sécurité de l'esprit? Pour l'esprit, la possibilité d'errer n'est-elle pas plutôt la contingence du bien?[18]

The surrealist imagination's process of disorientation and reorientation simultaneously builds and unravels the labyrinth, but since the labyrinthine "tissu capillaire" is necessary to unite the two worlds in which the surrealist finds elements for his combinations, the imagination must immediately enter a new field of unlimited possibility. In his efforts to clarify a surrealist method in the visual arts, Hans Holländer provides two visualizations of the creative process, which, he argues, are detectable in surrealist productions, especially those of Tanguy and Max Ernst: "The methods of inventing and finding unknown, not visible constellations from elements of reality reflect themselves as models in surrealist iconography. One of their leitmotifs is the labyrinth, another is the game of chess, and the two are connected."[19] The labyrinth, like the chessboard, presents a field of vast possibility, and it is this quality, as well as its ability to fuse contradictions, to muddle the ideas of interiority and exteriority, of progress and stasis, beginning and ending, that renders the labyrinth a useful metaphor for the dialectic at the heart of surrealist aesthetics.

Thus far, the form of the labyrinth as it develops in "La Maison d'Yves" has been regarded as a visualization of surrealist consciousness, of the Surrealist's way of seeing as it is acted upon in his creative production. To leave off here, and thus to limit the implications of the labyrinth to the realm of artistic creation, would be to insult Breton's vision of Surrealism. Breton viewed the movement not only as a revolution in artistic consciousness, but also as a participant in a revolution in political conscience. Although Surrealism had broken with the Communist party by the time Breton composed "La Maison d'Yves," the movement maintained much of its revolutionary fervor, and a commitment to social change, perhaps even a utopian vision, is articulated in particular images in the poem.

The mythological figures named in the poem — Ariane, the Argonaut, and Theseus, who is implied in the "vous" — are all associated with an adventurous quest for the marvelous. In the case of Theseus, the marvelous is the Minotaur; for the Argonaut it is the Golden Fleece. The original myths in which these figures appear are folded into the labyrinth of the poem. Beyond the somewhat facile analogy of the quest lie the implications of the myths themselves: one must consider the social conditions within which these quests were undertaken. In the case of these two stories, the quest for the marvelous is an effort to effect liberating social change: the capture of the Golden Fleece permits Jason to unseat his pretender uncle; Theseus's victory over the Minotaur frees Athens from its terrible annual tribute of human lives to the government of Crete. Breton's particular adaptation of the Theseus myth in "La Maison d'Yves" retains the ultimate goal of the quest – liberation from tyranny – but changes the terms of the adventure.

It has already been noted that the Surrealists could not view the figure of the Minotaur as a wholly negative force. (The Minotaur itself is an instance of radical recombination.) For the Surrealists the beast embodies the elements of the unconscious and the unknown, inhabiting the inviting and yet threatening world of dream. Associated thus with "le monde intérieur," the Minotaur in the surrealist myth is not so much imprisoned by the labyrinth as connected via the labyrinth to "le monde extérieur." In the poem, as was noted above, Ariane is enclosed, "dans sa chambre étui." Perhaps the "chambre étui," like the "lassos" and "jambages," offers a description of the poem itself – it is not outside the bounds of surrealist imagination to picture a labyrinth of vast possibilities reduced to a tiny box – so that Ariane, like Theseus, is within the labyrinth. This implies that the guiding line does not lead *out of* the maze, but itself originates *in* the maze – for it was Ariane who provided Theseus with the skein of thread – and can lead only back into the maze. So it is with the reader: upon reaching what he considers the end of the poem he finds himself at the beginning: the final line loops back to the first. As figured in "La Maison d'Yves," the surrealist Theseus, the revolutionary, does not free the world from tyranny by entering the labyrinth and destroying the beast, but by taking the entire world into the labyrinth with him, where, confounded with the liberated unconscious, the world is transformed and "l'homme" is released from "le tour des objets dont il a été amené à faire usage, et que lui a livrés sa nonchalance, ou son effort, son effort presque toujours, car il a consenti à travailler. . . ."[20] The labyrinth of "La Maison d'Yves" can be seen, then, not only as a "communicating vessel" joining the interior and exterior worlds for the purpose of the production of art, but as a region of consciousness in which the two worlds of human experience are combined so that the outside world, the political realm, is changed for the better as it is assumed into the structure of a revolutionary, freedom-affirming imagination.

"La Maison d'Yves" is much more than Breton's playful tribute to a fellow Surrealist: not only does it stand as an exemplar of Breton's verbal artistry, but it articulates, more through its intrinsic structure than by direct statement, the theoretical foundations and social conscience of the movement of which it is a product. "La Maison" is a communicating labyrinth within which the external world and the internal realm of dream are intertwined, and in which, in turn, the reader is confounded. As such it may serve as an emblem of "l'intuition *poétique* . . . débridée dans le surréalisme," which, Breton writes in a late essay,[21] "se veut non seulement assimilatrice de toutes les formes connues mais hardiment créatrice de nouvelles formes – soit en posture d'embrasser toutes les structures du monde, manifesté ou non. Elle seule nous pourvoit du fil qui remet sur le chemin de la Gnose, en tant que connaissance de la Réalité suprasensible, 'invisiblement visible dans un éternel mystère.'"

Notes

1. André Breton, "Ce que Tanguy voile et révèle," in André Breton, *Yves Tanguy* (New York: Pierre Matisse Editions, 1946), 35.

2. Composed between 1935 and 1940. Collected in André Breton, *Poèmes* (Paris: Éditions Gallimard, 1948), 139. All further references to "La Maison d'Yves" will be to the poem as it appears in this edition.

3. André Breton, *Les Vases communicants* (Paris: Éditions Gallimard, 1955), 161.

4. Hans Holländer provides a cogent and interesting discussion of labyrinths in general and surrealistic labyrinths in particular in "Ars inventendi et investigandi: zur surrealistischen Methode," *Wallraf-Richartz Jahrbuch* 32 (1970), 222–30.

5. See Holländer, 223.

6. Published in *Minotaure* 1 (1933).

7. See *Yves Tanguy Retrospective 1925–1955* (Paris: Centre Georges Pompidou, 1982), 118 and 123.

8. Holländer develops the idea of the labyrinthine *"Raum,"* as well as that of the "danger" of the labyrinth with a consideration of time as it relates to maze structures.

9. Picasso's rendition of the Minotaur was the first to appear on the cover of the review. "C'est dans cette belle couverture que sortit, le 25 Mai 1933, le premier numéro de *Minotaure.* Par la suite – comme jadis Thésée – Derain, Matisse, Miró, André Masson, Magritte, Salvador Dali se mesurèrent avec la créature fabuleuse, chacun donnant sa version du monstre pour la couverture de la revue." Brassaï, *Conversations avec Picasso,* quoted in *Picasso: Metamorphoses et unité,* ed. Jean Leymarie (Geneva: Editions d'Art Albert Skira, 1971), 251.

10. Brief discussions of this ambivalence can be found in Mary Ann Caws, *André Breton* (New York: Twayne Publishers, 1971), 16 and 80.

11. The images of wounding and healing may well be related to the image of the "colin-maillard des blessures" in "Les Écrits s'en vont," also collected in *Poèmes,* 75, and to other similar images in Breton. The image of the wound recurs frequently in surrealist productions, both in literature and in visual art. See also Mary Ann Caws, *The Poetry of Dada and Surrealism* (Princeton: Princeton University Press, 1970), 16.

12. Caws, *André Breton,* 46.

13. André Breton, *Manifestes du surréalisme* (Paris: Éditions Gallimard, 1963), 76–77.

14. Breton, *Vases communicants,* 161.

15. Ibid., 103.

16. Caws, *Poetry of Dada and Surrealism,* 79.

17. In Caws, *André Breton,* 46.

18. Breton, *Manifestes,* 13.

19. Holländer, 228.

20. Breton, *Manifestes,* 11.

21. "Du surréalisme en ses oeuvres vives," 1953, in *Manifestes,* 176.

Breton's *Ode à Charles Fourier* and the Poetics of Genre

Michel Beaujour

We have no reliable modern definition of *poetry*. This does not keep us from using freely such terms as *poeticalness, poetic language, poetic devices* and the like, as if we believed that the theoreticians who gave them currency were endowed with a mysterious *poetical competence* that enabled *them* (at least) to draw the line confidently between ordinary language, literary prose and poetry.

Unfortunately, theoreticians and the poets hardly agree as to what constitutes the poeticalness of poetry: we are faced with a Babel of poetics, and there is no transcendent arbiter to decide which is right.

Modern theories of poetry, including those that claim a (quasi-) scientific objectivity, are in fact ancillary to a given poetic practice. Clearly, Ezra Pound's influential dicta were bound up with his poetry; the Russian Formalists acknowledged their subordination to Futurism; and André Breton's Surrealism is rooted in his practice of "automatic writing." One could easily adduce a multitude of other examples of the solidarity between poetic practice and theory. It is less evident, but no less true, that a general semiotic of poetry, such as Jean Cohen's or Michael Riffaterre's,[1] derives from a "competence" achieved in the reading of a large corpus of texts that had previously been defined as "poetry."

Despite the unavoidable limitations of its competence, each poetics *must* nevertheless claim jurisdiction over "poetry" in general, so that in practice, each one of them ends up tailoring the "poetic canon" to fit the criteria that obtain in the primary corpus from which it extracted the distinctive features of "poeticalness" which it claims to be universal.

The overwhelming partiality of modern "poetics" for short lyrics and lexical features entails that, in practice, only discrete fragments of larger texts will be granted "poetic" status. In the French cultural context, Surrealism achieved hegemony largely because it foregrounded in its poetics what were then referred to as *images*, a term vaguely denoting a polymorphous entity which many Western poets and critics of the first half of this century claimed to be quintessentially "poetic." A salient characteristic of the *image* resides in its ability to be excerpted as a self-sufficient "poetic text," while longer texts are reputed to be "poetic" in proportion to their relative density in *images*. Though differing from other imagisms in its conception of the etiology and function of images, Surrealism shared with many other modernist tendencies a preference for short or "fragmentary" texts, as well as a marked disdain for traditional genres.

Ever since the abandonment of such "horizons of expectation" as were shared by poets and readers in the days when poetry was indeed "something written in a given poetic genre," it has become impossible, strictly speaking, to *read* those non-generic texts that are paratextually designated as "poetry." Whether this impossibility should be construed as progress is another matter: while readers who wish for reliable guidelines are at a loss, commentators, seeking to impose their authority upon the undecidable, thrive.

There are, however, modern texts that disregard some fundamental principles of modern poetics, including those upon which the writer himself had based his programmatic pronouncements. Such departures disconcert the critics who have adopted their poet's own poetics as the ultimate touchstone of poeticalness.

Some French modernist poets (Apollinaire, Cocteau, Aragon) built their careers on quick, brazen, doctrinal changes. Others, such as Breton, were careful to present their theoretical shifts as a dialectical progress. Although he abandoned "psychic automatism" after having championed it in his *First Manifesto*, Breton claimed it to be compatible with and embedded in the neo-romanticism and analogical occultism which he eventually formulated in the *Second Manifesto*. This relatively stable syncretism (sanctioned as it was by a long tradition) surely justified the pro-surrealist critic's attempt to use it as a reference with which to assess and interpret Breton's late poetry, even though the long poems of the forties often gave the slip to the critic's expectations. Still defending Breton's poetry against an alleged resistance of the public to "automatically" generated "images" and to dark occultist analogies, the encomiastic critics had to open an awkward second front against surrealistically competent readers who found Breton's long poems exceedingly prosaic and eloquent. Discrepancies between Breton's practice and his supposed theory were explained away with far-fetched references to surrealist poetics, or played down as trivial. The critic had to argue that, despite their apparent prosaism, Breton's poems were in fact poetic according to the very poetics imputed to Breton.

This may not be the best approach to Breton's *Ode à Charles Fourier*, whose "poetry" (if we define poeticalness as ungrammaticality, irrationality, analogical thought and semiosis undoing mimesis), is so manifestly overshadowed by eloquence, argument and grammaticality. It might be more sensible, since the title invites us to do so, to read the text as if it were indeed a panegyric ode to Charles Fourier. We would then be forced to displace the vexed question of poeticalness from the area of *lexis* and mimesis to that of genre: Breton's *Ode* is poetic because it displays generic features which belatedly, but pointedly, link it to an ancient tradition of praise, celebration and mourning. Evidently, shifting grounds will not allow us to answer the new question: but is it a good ode? The move merely enables us to see more clearly that the question of "poeticalness" can be posed within more than one framework, even when dealing with a contemporary text, if such a text somehow makes a generic claim.

The critics who have written at some length in defense of Breton's *Ode*, which they fear may not be a "poem," tend to believe, as does Gérald Schaeffer, that poems *qua* poems are allergic to "pure rationalism," and that, according to Anna Balakian, poems must not stoop to "straight philosophy."[2] If a poem is riddled with philosophical patches, it must redeem itself by "analogical thinking" or by its use of the "rhythms, images, analogies" that characterize "poetic language" according to surrealist poetics.[3] Ideas, obscured by images, then become mere epiphenomena of a more essential, if latent, lyricism. Schaeffer claims Breton's ode to be successful on this score:

En réalité . . . *l'Ode* ne se réduit pas à un texte de prose mal déguisé: les formules rhétoriques y tiennent une si grande, une si belle place qu'elles fondent précisément les assises architecturales analogues à celles que construit d'ordinaire la prosodie. Négligeant donc la technique du vers, nous nous appliquerons à l'analyse des formes d'ensemble et de détail, pour y découvrir un authentique lyrisme.[4]

In Schaeffer's discourse, as in much modern criticism, the verbal devices which he calls *formules rhétoriques* have been cut loose from the art of persuasion and from the art of (poetic) praise. The word *rhétorique* merely conjures up a bag of tricks: like magic spells, *rhetorical formulas* transmute base prose into poetic gold. Since eloquence has been condemned by modern poetics, the critic must deny or ignore that "rhetoric" bears any relation to it. An eloquent poem would be an "ill-disguised" piece of prose. Instead of acknowledging that poetry is in most respects a "second rhetoric," Schaeffer implicitly draws an ontological distinction between prose and "authentic lyricism." This dissociation enables the critic to ward off the scandalous realization that Breton turned to the epideictic mode of poetic eloquence in his long poems of the forties.

Nowhere is Breton's reversal (if indeed it was one for this master of eloquence) more manifest than in the *Ode à Charles Fourier*, the very title of which proclaims Breton's adoption of the poetic panegyric as a generic model, which he adapted to fit the ironic particulars of the situation.

According to the *Encyclopedia of Poetry and Poetics,* modern odes are "frequently the vehicle for public utterance on state occasions, as, for example, a ruler's birthday, accession, funeral, the unveiling or dedication of some imposing memorial or public work."[5] If such is the case, Breton's poem might well be called an anti-ode, since it starts with the recollection of a very unremarkable statue erected to the memory of a thinker – Charles Fourier – who had been so nearly forgotten that even Breton, familiar as he was with socialist and occultist writings, had known hardly anything about him before a chance encounter with his works in New York during the war.

Breton's *Ode*, then, is antithetical to occasional poetry written for performance within the ceremonial context of a dedication or unveiling. Breton could not have known at the time of writing that Fourier's statue had been removed from its pedestal during the German occupation of Paris: the epideictic poem happens to substitute for the inconspicuous monument evoked in its first lines. Instead of a glorious ruler, Fourier was only an obscure philosopher who had imagined a rulerless society regulated by the passions. But, as Jonathan Beecher notes in his recent biography of Fourier, Breton's *Ode* not only prepared the way for Michel Butor's and Roland Barthes's literary homages, and for a vigorous revival of Fourier studies in the post-war period; Breton's proselytism also enabled Fourier's utopia of passion and desire to influence the cultural critique that prepared the revolt of May 1968, when, at the behest of the Situationists, the visionary's statue was ceremoniously returned to its pedestal in the spot where, thirty years earlier, Breton had paid attention to it only when a pious, perhaps a pretty hand placed violets in centennial homage at its feet.[6]

Fourier's posthumous reputation and influence reached their nadir one hundred years after his death, at a time when the world was rushing into unprecedented barbarity. With his *Ode*, written in America at the end of the war, Breton marked the moment when Fourier's star almost imperceptibly started to rise again.

The striking efficacy of Breton's tribute may not be the least of the scandals attendant in his *Ode*, for it bespeaks an illocutionary force we no longer willingly impute to poetry, which we prefer to endow with vulnerability and powerlessness.

An intimate monologue, the *Ode* addresses the spirit of Fourier from the solitude of exile. Following a low-key anamnesis, the muffled utterance turns into a bleak report on the course of history and the state of the world in 1945, poles apart from Fourier's vision of harmony, which is eulogized in the final section of the *Ode*. A primer of Fourier's thought, the *Ode* can also be taken for the marginal comments of a reader who is still dizzy from the shock of recognizing in the works of an overlooked forerunner the very ideas towards which he had been forever groping. The resulting intertextuality of the *Ode* has long been recognized, and studied in detail.[7]

It is fitting that Breton should have written an ode, a panegyric ode, in order to celebrate Fourier's theory of the passions, for the ode is a *rhetori-*

cal genre (rather than a mimetic/narrative one) to the extent that it arises from an epideictic intent: all Western theories of persuasion draw their energy from an irradiating theory of the passions, those irrational drives the orator must arouse in order to achieve his ends.

Breton set Fourier's conception of the twelve "radical passions" at the center of his *Ode*. Divided into the passions that satisfy the yearnings of the five senses and those that foster the four *affections* (friendship, love, ambition, familism), the passionate order culminates in the synthetic, "distributive" or "mechanizing" passions: the *cabalist*, which underlies the "penchant for conspiring, calculating, forming combinations";[8] the *butterfly (la papillonne)*, or the desire for variety and contrast; and the *composite* that seeks its satisfaction in a combination of sensual and spiritual delights.

This is not the proper place for a discussion of Fourier's radical and interesting departures from such previous theoreticians of the passions as (*inter alii*) Aristotle, Thomas Aquinas and Descartes. Suffice it to mention that the passions were usually considered to be dangerous motions of the human soul responding to inner or outer stimuli: the man of wisdom endeavored to know and control his passions, while the rhetor studied them in order to mimic their manifestations in his eloquence, and to arouse them in his audience. Fourier, on the other hand, described a possible world where the passions, satisfied and tempered in work, leisure, and social intercourse, would fuel the mechanisms of a diverse yet harmonious society. *Harmony* was to redeem at last the negative essence of rhetorical persuasion, by doing away with a need that had been bound up with the old conflictual social order. By the same token, the quest for glory which motivates the writing of epideictic odes would be transmuted, for the people in Harmony would have no need to lavish praise on extraordinary individuals. Praise would be mutual, true and fair, as all passions found their outlet, and their match.

Breton's report to the spirit of Fourier on the calamitous debasement of the passions in 1945 takes up the center of his *Ode:* it comprises a segment that the reader is manifestly invited to call the *antistrophe* by the odd but explicit markers that frame it. The first one, made up of two separate and opposed semicircles of lettering forming an incomplete horizontal *S* shape, reads: *Ici j'ai renversé la vapeur poétique*, while the second, a horizontal *S* line, wordlessly echoes the first one. These two reversals of the poetic energy evoke the alternation of *strophe, antistrophe* and *epode* in the Pindaric ode, which may have textually encoded the to-and-fro motion of the chorus during its public performance.

The symbolic, or analogical, significance of this turn and return was belatedly made explicit by Macrobius in his *Commentary on the Dream of Scipio* (2.3): "As is imitated in the strophe the forward motion of the starry sphere, so in the antistrophe the reversion imitates the retrograde course of the planets." If such is the case, then, any ode containing strophe and antistrophe rests on a cosmic analogy and is, to that extent, analogous to Fourier's own thought, which is steeped in cosmological correspondences, as also was Breton's later version of Surrealism.

We now see that if one wants to save Breton's poem for "poetry" by showing that it is "analogical" rather than discursively dialectical, one might as well pay attention to the generic characteristics which formally motivate whatever system of analogies might be sought at the level of its so-called *images*. In fact, Breton's choice of the ode, and this genre's congruence with his own and Fourier's cosmic analogy, sets the scene for a *mise en abîme* which cannot be noticed by the critic who willfully overlooks generic markers, or merely finds in them the signs of a modernist irony toward genre.

Whether we approach it from the point of view of epideictic rhetoric (in which case Fourier's transmutation of the passions from nasty psychic predicaments into the prime movers of Harmony becomes the very rationale for Breton's return to prophetic eloquence), or in the context of a genre that encodes a latent cosmic view, Breton's *Ode* turns out to be allergic to reductive strictures that define poetry as a numinous kind of ungrammaticality. An awareness of the generic and rhetorical matrix allows one to correct the categorical mistake which lodges the poetry of *Ode* in microscopic lexical features rather than in the macroscopic interaction of epideixis with the traditional symbolism of the ode.

The question concerning *Ode à Charles Fourier* and other long modern "poems" devoid of striking lexical deviances or "mimetic incongruities" (I'm thinking particularly of those "poems" that build an argument or develop a speech act, such as *praise*) proves to be not so much whether they contain a mixture of "poetry" and "prose," but whether the question makes any sense at all, given the theoretical emperor's state of undress.

Have we then reached an agreement with Michael Riffaterre's claim that genre—in this case, the ode—*produces* poetic ungrammaticalities: "The genre, because it is a grammar, reorders the words and destroys or threatens their connotations in the language. Hence the obscurity . . . the genre structure is transforming the mimetic into the symbolic."[9] Do we believe that the poem "makes sense only when read as a metonymy of the whole genre"[10]? If what is meant is that only those readers who know something about odes can understand, in a general sort of way, an ode, even such an odd one as Breton's, and that those who do not know necessarily misconstrue the text in some respects, one must indeed agree. But one may doubt that in a predominantly argumentative and eloquent genre, as opposed to a mimetic and/or narrative one, the criterion of mimetic subversion through generic intertextuality can be used to determine, assess or even describe the poeticalness of the text. If a generic matrix or grammar did necessarily produce "poetry" (in the sense of disturbed mimesis and specific ungrammaticalities), genre, as a type, would indeed determine the "poeticalness" of each of its tokens. Leaving aside the inconvenient fact that some genres generate literary prose-texts that have little claim to "poeticalness" in the sense of a deviance from the grammar of the language, it appears that the generic grammar does produce more or less well-formed tokens of the genre, which may strike the modern reader as quite "poetic," or hardly "poetic" at all.

Recognizing genre leaves the reader in a quandary as to whether the text is "poetic" in part or *in toto:* there is progress in understanding, but none in the matter of assessing "poeticalness," unless one can enforce the principle, and this seems to be the only logical issue, that genericity makes poetry because one says so, by reference perhaps to some ancient pragmatic context that commanded, in certain circumstances that have been weakly encoded in the generic grammar handed down to us, the use of certain speech styles and performance features such as verse, song or dance, that unfortunately fail to occur in most modern realizations. In short, genre, at least in the case of ancient and worn-out types, offers not so much a horizon of expectation and a surefire poetic matrix as a scholarly mirage. Genre is a poor guide to the recognition of "poetry," if such a thing does exist independently of naive beliefs, learned competence, and authoritarian assertions. Yet it gives something to hold on to, something specific to talk about.

Pity the modern critic who has taken for an unshakable *terminus a quo* the romantic critique and subversion of the traditional generic taxonomies that have brought about the simplistic dichotomy between a transgeneric genre called *poetry,* and a grab bag called *literary discourse* or *literature (tout le reste est littérature . . .).*[11] He will henceforth take those generic designations that sometimes appear in the paratext of a "poem" to be ironic, playful, or grossly retrograde. For him, *epic* and *ode* are quaint, perhaps provocative markers that have nothing to do with the essence of the poetic, which is beyond genre and in any case must shatter such mundane restraints.

Thus, Gérald Schaeffer's long interpretative commentary on Breton's text uses the word *ode* several times, but only as a short title. Schaeffer conspicuously fails to note in any way that the *Ode* is an ode, so that the striking iconic markers separating the antistrophe from the strophe and the epode receive a minimum of attention and strictly as the boundaries separating Breton's "own text" from his "borrowings" from Fourier. This sort of distracted misreading, one suspects, results from a well-intentioned eagerness to rehabilitate the poem as "poetry," if not quite as "pure poetry," then at least as lyrical poetic analogy. But Schaeffer would not have been much better off had he recognized the manifestations of a generic grammar in the poem. He would merely have concluded, as I have above, that it was, indeed, an ode. He would have understood a little better why the text was structured as it is. But he would not have progressed one step beyond his belief that there is an essential antagonism between *poetry* and *pure rationalism*. It seems that at the end of his poetic career, Breton realized the absurdity of such ideological distinctions, a realization which he inscribed in the stylistic indifferentiation of his long poems and particularly in his *Ode à Charles Fourier*.

Notes

1. Jean Cohen, *Le Haut Langage: Théorie de la poéticité* (Paris: Flammarion, 1979). Michael Riffaterre, *Semiotics of Poetry* (Bloomington and London: Indiana University Press, 1978).

2. Gérald Schaeffer, "Un petit matin de 1937," in Marc Eigeldinger, ed., *André Breton* (Neuchâtel: La Baconnière, 1970), 265; Anna Balakian, *André Breton, Magus of Surrealism* (New York: Oxford University Press, 1971), 197.

3. Schaeffer, 265.

4. Ibid., 249.

5. Preminger, Warnke, and Hardison, eds., *Encyclopedia of Poetry and Poetics* (Princeton: Princeton University Press, 1965), 585.

6. Jonathan Beecher, *Charles Fourier: The Visionary and His World* (Berkeley: University of California Press, 1986), 3; Michel Butor, *La Rose des Vents. 32 Rhumbs pour Charles Fourier* (Paris, 1970); Roland Barthes, *Sade, Fourier, Loyola* (Paris, 1971).

7. André Breton, *Ode à Charles Fourier,* introduction and notes by Jean Gaulmier (Paris: Klincksieck, 1961); Emile Letouck, "La lecture surréaliste de Charles Fourier," *Australian Journal of French Studies* 20, 1 (1983), 26–36.

8. Beecher, 227.

9. Riffaterre, 160–61. Elsewhere, we read: ". . . the genre *has* a grammar and this grammar merely develops a very limited number of matrix sentences" (emphasis added, 154).

10. Ibid., 163.

11. See my "Genus universum" in *Glyph* 7 (1980), 15–31.

André Breton: A Selective Bibliography, 1971-1988

The following bibliography attempts to continue to the present Michael Sheringham's *André Breton: A Bibliography* (London: Grant & Cutler), which is indispensable and very complete for the period up to 1971.

The first two sections of the present bibliography list works by Breton: first publications, reprints and translations. The third and fourth sections include secondary material: monographs, dissertations, parts of books and journal articles. Only studies that specifically focus on Breton and his works are included. Thus, most of the books and articles on general aspects of Surrealism are omitted, although they often refer to Breton.

I am indebted to two recent, ongoing bibliographies on Surrealism: *Signes,* which is a newsletter and bibliography published four times a year by the members of Champs des activités surréalistes, and Michel Carassou's annual bibliography in *Mélusine.*

I would like to thank Dan Cristea for his help and June Fischer for her superb typing.

Rudolf E. Kuenzli

I. Works by Breton – Separate Publications

Breton, André. *L'Amour fou.* Trans. Ferdinando Albertazzi. Turin: Einaudi, 1974.

———. *Il Cadavere squisito, la sua esaltazione.* Ed. Arturo Schwarz. Milan: Galleria Schwarz, 1975 [exhibition catalog].

———. *Mad Love.* Trans. Mary Ann Caws. Lincoln: University of Nebraska Press, 1987.

———. *Manifestes du surréalisme.* Trans. into Japanese by Jun Ebara. Tokyo: Haku-suisha, 1982.

———. *Manifestos do surrealismo.* Trans. Luis Forbes. Sao Paulo: Editora Brasiliense, 1985.

———. *Nadja.* Trans. Giordano Falzoni. Turin: Einaudi, 1977.

———. *Oeuvres complètes.* Bibliothèque de la Pléiade. Ed. Marguerite Bonnet. Vol. 1. Paris: Gallimard, 1988.

———. *Poems of André Breton.* Trans. Jean-Pierre Cauvin and Mary Ann Caws. Austin: University of Texas Press, 1982.

———. *Poesie.* Trans. Giordano Falzoni. Turin: Einaudi, 1977.

———. *Ou'est-ce que le surréalisme?* Cognac: Actuel/Le temps qu'il fait, 1986 [reprint].

———. *Surrealism and Painting.* Trans. Simon Watson Taylor. New York: Harper & Row, 1972.

———. *What Is Surrealism?: Selected Writings.* Ed. Franklin Rosemont. New York: Monad Press, 1978.

———. *What Is Surrealism?* Trans. David Gascoyne. New York: Haskell House Publishers, 1974.

———, ed. *Almanach surréaliste du demi-siècle.* Paris: Plasma, 1978 [reprint].

Breton, André, and Philippe Soupault. *Les Champs magnétiques.* Trans. into Hungarian by Jean Paranes. Budapest: Magvetö, 1984.

———. *The Magnetic Fields.* Trans. David Gascoyne. London: Atlas, 1985.

———. *Le Manuscrit des "Champs magnétiques."* Ed. Serge Fauchereau. Paris: Lachenal and Ritter, 1984.

Breton, André, et al. *L'Affaire Barrès.* Ed. Marguerite Bonnet. Paris: José Corti, 1987.

———. *Secret Affinities: Words and Images by René Magritte.* Houston: Institute for the Arts, Rice University, 1977 [exhibition catalog].

———. *Tracts surréalistes et déclarations collectives (1922–1969).* Ed. José Pierre. Paris: Le Terrain Vague, 1980.

II. Works by Breton – Individual Poems, Essays, Letters

Breton, André. "As in a Wood." In *The Shadow and Its Shadow,* ed. Paul Hammond. London: British Film Institute, 1978.

———. "Baya." *Pleine Marge,* 6 (December 1987), 91–93.

———. "Ça commence bien!" In *Documents relatifs à la fondation de l'Internationale situationiste,* ed. G. Berreby. Paris: Allia, 1985.

———. "Deux poèmes de jeunesse, présentés par Marguerite Bonnet." *Création,* 15 (1979).

———. "Etourdissent . . . y compris par lui-même." In *Les Critiques de notre temps et Aragon.* Ed. Bernard Lecherbonnier. Paris: Garnier, 1976, pp. 20–22.

———. "The Faces of Women." In *Man Ray: The Photographic Image,* Ed. Janus. Woodbury, N.Y.: Barron's, 1980.

———. "Inédits." In André Breton, *Oeuvres complètes.* Ed. Marguerite Bonnet. Paris: Gallimard, 1988, I, 29–47, 489–638, 1033–62.

———. "Lâchez tout." *Adam International Review,* 41, no. 404–6 (1978), 31–32 [unpublished poem]

———. "Lettres de 1942 et 1943 à Alain Bosquet." In *Alain Bosquet.* Paris: Belfond, 1979, 137–39.

———. "Note sur les masques à transformation de la côte pacifique Nord-Ouest." *Pleine Marge,* 1 (May 1985), 7–15.

———. "Les pages marquées de craie . . . ." *Modernités,* 1 (1986).

———. "Photography Is Not Art." In *Man Ray, the Photographic Image,* Ed. Janus. Woodbury, N.Y.: Barron's, 1980.

———. "Réunion du 23 janvier 1925 au Bar Certà; Jeanne d'Arc." *Luna-Park,* 8–9 (1986), 5–6.

———. "Taking Stock of Surrealism." *Vie des Arts,* 80, no 2 (1975), 16–17.

———. "Trois textes signalés par Gérard Roche." *Champs des activités surréalistes,* 17 (February 1983), 20–38.

———. "Une conscience si nette . . ." [text of 3 January 1916 to Thédore Fraenkel]. *Digraphe,* 30 (June 1983), 27–29.

———. "Une révolution totale de l'objet." *XXe Siècle,* 42, no. 36 (1974), 131.

———. "We don't ear it that way." In *Dictionnaire général du surréalisme et de ses environs,* Ed. Adam Biron and René Passeron. Fribourg: Office du Livre, 1982.

Breton, André, and Benjamin Péret. "Si le surréalisme était maître de Paris." In Goutier, Jean Michel. *Benjamin Péret.* Paris: H. Veyrier, 1982.

Breton, André, and Philippe Soupault. "Pages retrouvées des *Champs magnétiques.*" *Digraphe,* 30 (June 1983), 33–47.

———. *If You Please.* In *Dada Performance,* ed. Mel Gordon. New York: PAJ Publications, 1987.

Breton, André, and Léon Trotsky. "Pour un art révolutionnaire indépendant." *Pleine Marge,* 3 (May 1986), 76–84.

III. Secondary Literature – Monographs and Dissertations

Alexandrian, Sarane. *André Breton par lui-même.* Paris: Editions du Seuil, 1971.

———. *André Breton.* Paris: Seuil, 1977.

Ariew, Robert. "La Thématique de 'Poisson soluble': Etude cybernétique." Diss. University of Illinois, 1975.

Asari, Makoto. *André Breton et le sacré. Essai sur Breton selon quelques textes religieux.* Paris: Publications de l'Université Paris III, 1984.

Balakian, Anna. *André Breton: Magus of Surrealism.* New York: Oxford University Press, 1971.

Barck, Karlheinz, ed. *Surrealismus in Paris 1919–1939.* Leipzig: Reclam, 1986.

Béhar, Henri, and Michel Carassou. *Le Surréalisme.* Paris: Le Livre de poche, 1984.

Binni, Lanfranco. *Breton.* Florence: La nuova Italia, 1971.

———. *Quattro studi francesi: Lesage, Diderot, Zola, Breton.* Rome: Bulzoni, 1979.

Biro, Adam, and René Passeron. *Dictionnaire général du surréalisme et de ses environs.* Fribourg: Office du Livre, 1982.

Bonnet, Marguerite. *André Breton: Naissance de l'aventure surréaliste.* Paris: Corti, 1975.

———, ed. *Les Critiques de notre temps et Breton.* Paris: Garnier, 1974.

Bonnet, Marguerite, Jacqueline Chénieux-Gendron, and José Pierre. *Revues surréalistes françaises autour d'André Breton, 1948–1972.* Millwood, N.Y.: Kraus International Publications, 1982.

Bürger, Peter, ed. *Surrealismus.* Darmstadt: Wissenschaftliche Buchgesellschaft, 1982.

Carassou, Michel. *Jacques Vaché et le groupe de Nantes.* Paris: J.-M. Place, 1986.

Cardinal, Roger. *Breton: "Nadja."* London: Grant and Cutler, 1986.

Cardoza y Aragón, Luis. *André Breton: atisbado sin la mesa parlante.* Mexico: Universidad Nacional Autónoma de México, 1982.

Carrouges, Michel. *André Breton and the Basic Concepts of Surrealism.* Trans. Maura Pendergast. University: Univ. of Alabama Press, 1974.

Caws, Mary Ann. *André Breton.* New York: Twayne Publishers, 1971.

Chénieux-Gendron, Jacqueline. *Le Surréalisme et le roman.* Lausanne: L'Age d'Homme, 1983.

———. *Le Surréalisme.* Paris: Presses universitaires de France, 1984.

Crastre, Victor. *André Breton, trilogie surréaliste, "Nadja," "Les Vases communicants," "L'Amour fou."* Paris: Société d'édition d'enseignement supérieur, 1971.

Crespi, Marcantonio. *"Nadja et L'Amour fou:* les textes communicants d'André Breton." Diss. Rutgers University, 1987.

Cuto, José Geraldo. *André Breton. A transparência do sonho.* São Paulo: Ed. Brasiliense, 1984.

Dickinson, Richard T. "The Animal Metamorphoses of André Breton." Diss. New York University, 1983.

Ellenwood, William R. "André Breton and Freud." Diss. Rutgers University, 1972.

Facioli, Valentin. *André Breton, Léon Trotski. Por una arte revolucionaria independente.* Trans. C.S. Guedes and R. Bonaventura. Rio de Janeiro: Paz et Terra, 1985.

Finkelstein, Haim. *Surrealism and the Crisis of the Object.* Ann Arbor: UMI Research Press, 1979.

Fontanella, Luigi. *Il surrealismo italiano.* Rome: Bulzoni, 1983.

Gabellone, Lino. *L'Oggetto surrealista: il testo, la città, l'oggetto in Breton.* Turin: G. Einaudi, 1977.

Galateria, Daria. *Invito alla lettura di André Breton.* Milan: Mursia, 1977.

Gerant, Mary-Kathleen. "Movement, Rest, and Metamorphosis: An Essay on the Poetics of André Breton." Diss. Univ. of North Carolina, 1979.

Gibson, Jennifer Ann. "Surrealism's Early Maps of the Unconscious." Diss. University of Virginia, 1985.

Giménez-Frontín, J.L. *El Surrealismo: en torno al movimento bretoniano.* Barcelona: Montesinos, 1983.

Goldstein, Lisa. *The Dream Years.* New York: Bantam, 1985 [fiction].

Green, Leslie Anne. "Mythes et archétypes dans une oeuvre surréaliste: *Poisson soluble* d'André Breton." Diss. Northwestern University, 1981.

Guillaume, Paul, ed. *Sculptures nègres. Collection André Breton et Paul Éluard.* New York: Hacker Art Books, 1973.

Hanson, Marja W. "Paradox and Contradiction: André Breton's Problems in Defining Surrealism." Diss. Johns Hopkins University, 1975.

Higgins, Ian, ed. *Surrealism and Language.* Edinburgh: Scottish Academic Press, 1986.

Hozzel, Malte. *Bild und Einheitswirklichkeit im Surrealismus: Eluard und Breton.* Frankfurt am Main: Lang, 1980.

Lamy, Suzanne. *André Breton: hermétisme et poésie dans "Arcane 17."* Montreal: Presses de l'Université de Montréal, 1977.

Lang, Carol. "The Surrealist Novel: Its Principles and Structures in André Breton's *Nadja, L'Amour fou* and *Arcane 17."* Diss. Univ. of Arizona, 1981.

Lavergne, Philippe. *André Breton et le mythe.* Paris: J. Corti, 1985.

Legrand, Gérard. *André Breton en son temps.* Paris: Soleil Noir, 1976.

————. *Breton.* Paris: Belfond, 1977.

Lemaître, Maurice. *Sur Tristan Tzara, André Breton, Philippe Soupault . . . .* Paris: Centre de Créativité, 1980.

Lenk, Elisabeth. *Der springende Narziss: André Bretons poetischer Materialismus.* Munich: Rogner and Bernhard, 1971.

Margoni, Iros. *Per conoscere André Breton e il surrealismo.* Milan: Mondadori, 1976.

Matic, D. *André Breton oblique.* Montpellier: Fata Morgana, 1976.

Matthews, J.H. *Towards the Poetics of Surrealism.* Syracuse, N.Y.: Syracuse Univ. Press, 1976.

————. *The Imagery of Surrealism.* Syracuse, N.Y.: Syracuse Univ. Press, 1977.

————. *Surrealism, Insanity and Poetry.* Syracuse, N.Y.: Syracuse Univ. Press, 1982.

————. *André Breton: Sketch for an Early Portrait.* Amsterdam, Philadelphia: J. Benjamins, 1986.

Mercurio, Vittorino. *Le Roman surréaliste: Nadja. Essai d'interprétation.* Cagliari: Dattena, 1979.

Michelon, Valérie. "A Translation of André Breton's *Nadja* with Critical Introduction." M.A. Thesis, University of Oklahoma, 1987.

Mor, Samuel. "An Inquiry Into Madness: The Meaning of Madness in the Works of Virginia Woolf, André Breton, and Y.H. Bremer." Diss. University of Southern California, 1979.

Mourier-Casile, Pascaline. *André Breton, explorateur de la mère-moire: Trois lectures d' "Arcane 17," texte palimpseste.* Paris: Presses universitaires de France, 1986.

Navarri, Roger. *André Breton, 'Nadja.'* Paris: Presses universitaires de France, 1986.

Nessen, Susan Weil. "Surrealism in Exile: The Early New York Years, 1940–42." Diss. Boston University, 1986.

Palazón Mayoral, María Rosa. "Reflexiones sobre estética a partir de André Breton." Diss. México: Universidad Nacional Autónoma de México, 1986.

Parmentier, Michael. "De l'aliénation à l'intégration dans la pensée d'André Breton: La relation à soi, à la gemme, à la communauté humaine et au monde." Diss. University of Toronto, 1979.

Pierre, José. *Surréalisme et anarchie.* Paris: Plasma, 1983.

————. *L'Univers surréaliste.* Paris: Somogy, 1983.

————. *1 'Aventure surréaliste autour d'André Breton.* Paris: Filipacchi, 1986 [exhibition catalog].

————. *Changer la vue. André Breton et la révolution surréaliste du regard.* Cahors: Musée de Cahors, 1986 [exhibition catalog].

————. *André Breton et la peinture.* Lausanne: L'Age d'Homme, 1987.

Pillet, Alain-Pierre, ed. *André Breton à Venice.* Geneva: Iles Célèbes, 1984.

Plouvier, Paule. *Poétique de l'amour chez André Breton.* Paris: Corti. 1983.

Ramet, Robert. "The Interrelation of Politics and Poetry as Seen in the Works of André Breton and Pablo Neruda." Diss. University of California, Berkeley, 1977.

Rosello, Mireille. *L'Humour noir selon André Breton.* Paris: José Corti, 1987.

Rosemont, Franklin. *André Breton and the First Principles of Surrealism.* London: Pluto Press, 1978.

Saporta, Marc, ed. *André Breton ou le surréalisme, même.* Lausanne: L'Age d'Homme, 1988.

Sayegh, Alia. "The Concept and Role of Woman in the Works of André Breton." Diss. University of Pennsylvania, 1974.

Scheerer, Thomas M. "Textanalytische Studien zur 'écriture automatique.' " Diss. Universität Bonn, 1974.

Schwarz, Arturo. *André Breton, Trotsky et l'anarchie.* Paris: Union Général d'Editions, 1976.

Sheringham, Michael. *André Breton: A Bibliography.* London: Grant & Cutler, 1972.

Steinwachs, Ginka. *Mythologie des Surrealismus: oder Die Rückverwandlung von Kultur in Natur.* Basel: Stroemfeld/Roter Stern, 1985.

Stultz, Janice *"Poisson soluble,* the Poetic Quest of André Breton." Diss. Princeton Univ., 1977.

Vielwahr, André. *Sous le signe des contradictions: André Breton de 1913 à 1924.* Paris: Nizet, 1980.

Violato, Gabriella. *Scriture surrealiste.* Rome: Bulzoni, 1982.

Virmaux, Alain, and Odette Virmaux. *André Breton, qui êtes-vous?* Lyon: La Manufacture, 1987.

Vogt, Ulrich. *Le point noir. Politik und Mythos bei André Breton.* Frankfurt am Main, Bern: Peter Lang, 1982.

IV. Secondary Literature – Articles and Parts of Books

Abastado, Claude. "Ecriture automatique et instance du sujet." *Revue des Sciences Humaines,* 4, no. 184 (1981), 59–75.

Abel, Lionel. "The Surrealists in New York." *Commentary,* 72, no. 4 (October 1981), 44–54.

Ablamowicz, Aleksander. "La Structure du romanesque dans *Nadja* d'André Breton." In *Signes du roman, signes de la transition,* ed. Jean Bessière. Paris: Presses universitaires de France, 1986.

Albersmeier, Franz-Josef. "Collage und Montage im surrealistischen Roman: zu Aragons *Le Paysan de Paris* und Bretons *Nadja." Zeitschrift für Literaturwissenschaft und Linguistik,* 46 (1982).

Alexandrian, Sarane. "La Psychanalyse et le rêve." In *André Breton ou le surréalisme, même,* ed. Marc Saporta. Lausanne: L'Age d'Homme, 1988, 154–62.

Allen, Suzanne. "L'impossible distance." *Revue d'Esthétique,* 1–2 (1979), 272–96.

Amprimoz, Alexandre. "Note sur l'ouverture des *Pas perdus." Les Lettres Romanes,* 36, no. 2 (May 1982), 149–56.

Antoine, Régis. "André Breton et les mondes noirs." *L'Afrique Littéraire,* 58 (1981), 58–70.

Ariew, Robert. "André Breton's *Poisson soluble.*" *Association for Literary and Linguistic Computing Bulletin,* 6, 34–41.

Arrouye, Jean. "La Photographie dans *Nadja.*" *Mélusine,* 4 (1983), 123–51.

Aspley, Keith. "André Breton's Poems for Denise." *French Studies,* 41 (January 1987), 52–61.

———. " 'La Grèce n'a jamais existé': Myth, Legend, and Ritual in the Writings of André Breton." In *Myth and Legend in French Literature,* ed. K. Aspley, D. Bellos, and P. Sharratt. London: Modern Humanities Research Association, 1982.

Avni, Ora. "Breton et l'idéologie: Machine à coudre-parapluie." *Littérature* (Paris, France), 51 (1983), 15–27.

Balakian, Anna. "André Breton and Psychiatry." In *Medicine and Literature.* Ed. Enid Peschel. New York: Watson, 1980, 160–170.

———. " 'Au Regard des divinités': modèle poétique de Breton." *Mélusine,* no. 1 (1979), 213–220.

———. "Breton and Drugs." *Yale French Studies,* 50 (1974), 96–107.

———. "Breton in the Light of Apollinaire." In *About French Poetry.* Ed. Mary Ann Caws. Detroit: Wayne State Univ. Press, 1974, 42–53.

———. "Fragments on Reality by Baudelaire and Breton." *New York Literary Forum,* no. 8–9, 101–109.

———. "From *Poisson soluble* to *Constellations:* Breton's Trajectory for Surrealism." *Twentieth Century Literature,* 21 (1975), 48–58.

Bancquart, Marie-Claire. "Lecture d'*Arcane 17.*" In *Le Surréalisme dans le texte.* Ed. Daniel Bougnoux. Grenoble: Pubs. de l'Univ. des Langues & Lettres de Grenoble, 1978, 281–292.

Baron, Pierre. "De Freud à Breton: entre la proie et l'ombre quelques aspects d'un héritage." *Champs des Activités Surréalistes,* 19 (1983).

Baude, Jeanne-Marie. "Culpabilité et valeurs morales selon André Breton." *Mélusine,* 8 (1986), 19–36.

———. "Transparence et opacité dans la poésie d'André Breton." *Mélusine,* no. 2 (1981), 117–129.

Bauer, Gerd. "Die Surrealisten und Sigmund Freud." *Jahresring* (1980–81), 139–54.

Beaujour, Michel. "La Poétique de l'automatisme chez André Breton." *Poétique,* 25 (1976), 116–123.

———. "Was ist *Nadja?*" In *Surrealismus,* ed. Peter Bürger. Darmstadt: Wissenschaftliche Buchgesellschaft, 1982.

Béhar, Henri. "L'Attraction passionnelle du théâtre." In *André Breton ou le surréalisme, même,* ed. Marc Saporta. Lausanne: L'Age d'Homme, 1988, 76–86.

Benamou, Michel. "Surrealist Writing: Metallic Feathers on a Soluble Fish." *Teaching Language through Literature,* 17, no. 1 (1977), 1–14.

Bersani, Jacques. "Le Champ du désespoir: Essai d'analyse de 'La Glace sans tain.' " In *Le Surréalisme dans le texte.* Ed. Daniel Bougnoux. Grenoble: Pubs. de l'Univ. des Langues & Lettres de Grenoble, 1978, 19–31.

Berranger, Marie-Paule. "Valéry corrigé par André Breton et Paul Éluard." *Pleine Marge,* 1 (May 1985), 103–6.

Bertrand, Jean-Pierre. " 'Littérature' (1919–1924) et l'institution littéraire: une double stratégie d'émergence." *Mélusine,* 8 (1986), 155–76.

Bertrand, Marc. "*Nadja:* Un secret de fabrication surréaliste." *L'Information Litté-raire,* 31 (1979), 82–90, 125–30.

Blachère, Jean-Claude. "Géographie physique et poétique de l'éden chez André Breton." *Mélusine,* 7 (1985), 100–17.

Bohn, Willard. "At the Cross-Roads of Surrealism: Apollinaire and Breton." *Kentucky Romance Quarterly,* 27 (1980), 85–96

———. "Semiosis and Intertextuality in Breton's 'Femme et oiseau.'" *Romantic Review,* 76, no. 4 (1985), 415–28.

Bonardel, Françoise. "Surréalisme et hermétisme." *Mélusine,* 2 (1981), 98–116.

Bonnet, Marguerite. "A partir de ces 'mécaniques à la fois naïves et véhementes . . . .'" *Pleine Marge,* 1 (May 1985), 18–28.

———. "A propos de l'*Introduction au discours sur le peu de réalité.*" In *Le Surréalisme dans le texte.* Ed. Daniel Bougnoux. Grenoble: Pubs. de l'Univ. des Langues & Lettres de Grenoble, 1978, 19–31.

———. "Trotsky et Breton." *Cahiers Léon Trotsky,* 25 (March 1986), 5–17.

Bonnet, Marguerite, and Etienne-Alain Hubert. "Sur deux types d'écriture sur-réaliste et leurs finalités dans *L'Immaculée Conception* d'André Breton et Paul Eluard." *Revue d'histoire littéraire de la France,* 5 (1987), 753–58.

Boulestereau, Nicole. "L'Épreuve de la nomination dans le premier manifeste du surréalisme." *Littérature,* 39 (1980), 47–53.

———"*Nadja* d'André Breton: entre le livre du désir et le désir du livre." *Littérales,* 1 (1986), 95–108.

Brandt, Per Aage. "The White-Haired Generator." *Poetics,* 6 (1972) 72–83.

Braun, Micheline Tison. "Scientist and Poet: Two Views of Chance." *Dada/Surrealism,* 7 (1977), 66–75.

Bremondy, Gisèle. "La grande promesse." In *André Breton ou le surréalisme, même,* ed. Marc Saporta. Lausanne: L'Age d'Homme, 1988, 135–40.

Bruno, Jean. "André Breton et l'expérience de l'illumination." *Mélusine,* 2 (1981), 53–69.

Butor, Michel, and Michel Launay. "Breton ou la grève des signes." In *Resistances, conversations aux antipodes.* Paris: Presses universitaires de France, 1983, 131–34.

Calas, Nicolas. "Freedom, Love and Poetry." *Artforum,* 22, no. 9 (May 1978), 22–27.

Carrouges, Marc. "La Dynamique de l'occultation." *Mélusine,* 2 (1981), 39–52.

Cassanyes, M. "Sobre l'exposició Picabia i la conferéncia de Breton." In *Francis Picabia.* Barcelona: Ministerio de Cultura, 1985 [exhibition catalog].

Cauvin, Jean-Pierre. "Literary Games of Chance: The André Breton." *Library Chronicle of The University of Texas,* 16 (1981), 16–41.

Caws, Mary Ann. "Dark Framing and the Analogical Ascent." *New York Literary Forum,* 4, 147–58.

———. "Notes on a Manifesto Style: 1924 Fifty Years Later." *The Journal of General Education,* 27 (1975), 88–90.

Champigny, Robert. "The First Person in *Nadja.*" In *About French Poetry.* Ed. Mary Ann Caws. Detroit: Wayne State University Press, 1974, 242–53.

Chapsal, Madeleine. "André Breton" [interview]. In her *Les Ecrivains en personne.* Paris: R. Julliard, 1975.

Chénieux-Gendron, Jacqueline. "André Breton: *Introduction au discours sur le peu de réalité.*" In *Le Surréalisme dans le texte.* Ed. Daniel Bougnoux. Grenoble: Pubs. de l'Univ. des Langues & Lettres de Grenoble, 1978, 129–45.

———. "Breton." *Dictionnaire des littératures de langue française.* Paris: Bordas, 1984, 1, 325–33.

———. "Breton, Leiris: l'espace forcené." In *Espace et poésie.* Ed. Michel Collot and Jean-Claude Mathieu. Paris: Presses de l'Ecole Normale supérieure, 1987.

———. "L'Expérience vive du récit." In *André Breton ou le surréalisme, même,* ed. Marc Saporta. Lausanne: L'Age d'Homme, 1988, 66–75.

———. "La Position du sujet chez Breton et Bataille." In *L'Objet au défi.* Ed. J. Chénieux-Gendron and M.-C. Dumas. Paris: Presses universitaires de France, 1987, 59–76.

———. "Pour une imagination pratique. André Breton: *Il y aura une fois . . .*" *L'Information Littéraire,* 24 (1972), 230–36.

Clébert, Jean-Paul. "Traces de Nadja: *Revue des Sciences Humaines,* 4, no. 184 (1981), 79–94.

Collier, Peter. "Dreams of a Revolutionary Culture: Gramsci, Trotsky and Breton." In *Visions and Blueprints: Avant-Garde Culture and Radical Politics in Early Twentieth-Century Europe,* ed. E. Timms and P. Collier. Manchester: Manchester University Press, 1988.

Cortanze, Gérard de. "Breton du côté de Guermantes." *Le Magazine littéraire,* 246 (October 1987), 39.

Cook, Albert. "Surrealism and Surrealisms." *The American Poetry Review,* 13, no. 4 (1984), 29–39.

Courtot, Claude. "Le Mercure et le soufre." In *André Breton ou le surréalisme, même,* ed. Marc Saporta. Lausanne: L'Age d'Homme, 1988, 56–65.

Cowling, Elizabeth. " 'Proudly we claim him as one of us': Breton, Picasso, and the Surrealist Movement." *Art History,* 8, no. 1 (1985).

Dachy, Marc. "Une aventure littéraire: le manuscript des *Champs magnétiques.*" *Le Magazine littéraire,* 213 (December 1984), 31.

Dahmer, Helmut. "Versäumte Lektionen: Aufsätze von André Breton in deutscher Übersetzung." *Psyche,* 36 (1983).

Décaudin, Michel. "Autour du premier manifeste." In *Surrealismo.* Quaderni del Novecento Francese 1. Rome: Bulzoni, 1974, 29–47.

Decottignies, Jean. "Le Poète et la statue." *Revue des Sciences Humaines,* 4, no. 184 (1981), 95–117.

Deguy, Michel. "André Breton: *Entretiens.*" *Cahiers du Chemin,* 19 (1973).

———. "Du *Signe ascendant* au sphynx vertébral. *Poétique,* 34 (April 1978), 226–40.

Desnos, Robert. "Lettre à André Breton" [4 April 1929]. In *Robert Desnos,* ed. Marie-Claire Dumas. Paris: Herne, 1987.

Dollé, Jean-Paul. "Breton et Freud." *Le Magazine littéraire,* no. 213 (December 1984), 35.

Drijkoningen, Fernand. "Comment lire un poème-objet." In *Le Plaisir de l'intertexte,* ed. R. Theis and H. Siepe. Frankfurt: Lang, 1986.

———. "De nacht van de helioptroop: Een surrealistisch model van lezen en interpreteren." *Forum der Letteren,* 6 (1979), 16–25.

Dunaway, John. "Maritain and Breton: Common Denominators in the Aesthetic Confrontation of Thomism and Surrealism." *French Literature Series*, 6 (1979), 16–25.

Durand, Pascal. "Pour une lecture institutionnelle du *Manifeste du surréalisme.*" *Mélusine*, 8 (1986), 177–95.

Durozoi, Gérard. "Breton, Péret et quelques autres." In *Benjamin Péret*, ed. Jean-Michel Goutier. Paris: H. Veyrier, 1982.

Eberz, Ingrid. "Kandinsky, Breton et le modèle purement intérieur." *Pleine Marge*, 1 (May 1985), 69–80.

Eckert, Norbert. "André Breton/Paul Eluard: *L'Immaculée Conception. Die unbefleckte Empfängnis.*" *Neue Deutsche Hefte*, 145 (1975), 189–90.

Eigeldinger, Marc. "André Breton et la lecture de Huysmans." In his *Mythologie et intertextualité*. Geneva: Slatkine, 1987.

————. "André Breton et le mythe de l'âge d'or." *Mélusine*, 7 (1985), 17–32.

————. "André Breton révélateur de Germain Nouveau." *Studi Francesi*, 73 (1981) 37–45.

————. "Poésie et langage alchimique chez André Breton." *Mélusine*, 2 (1981), 22–38.

Filliolet, Jacques. "Le Manifeste comme acte de discours: approches linguistiques." *Littérature*, 39 (October 1980), 23–28.

————. "Sur les routes du style." In *André Breton ou le surréalisme, même*, ed. Marc Saporta. Lausanne: L'Age d'Homme, 1988, 117–24.

Fontanella, L. "*Magnetic Fields*, the First Surrealist Work." *Terzo Occhio*, 12, no. 4 (1978), 1–9.

Fourny, Jean-François. "A propos de la querelle Breton-Bataille." *Revue d'Histoire Littéraire de la France*, 84, no. 3 (1984), 432–38.

Gaubert, Alain. "Crise de 'ver.'" *Licorne*, 8 (1984), 31–47.

————. "L'Enigme n'existe pas, ou: Ce que disait le groupe." *Licorne*, 9 (1985), 105–52.

Gaudin, Colette. "Tours et détours négatifs dans 'La Confession dédaigneuse' de Breton." *Romanic Review*, 71 (1980), 394–412.

Gavronsky, Serge. "Poétique de freinage: l'ambigu surréalisme." *La Revue des Lettres Modernes: Histoire des Idées et des Littératures*, 720–725 (1985), 21–38.

Geles, Dorina. "André Breton." *Steaua*, 23 (1972), 24–27.

Germain, Edward B. "Automatism and the Birth of Language." *Forum for Modern Language Studies*, 18, no. 2 (1982), 172–82.

Gibs, Sylwia. "Les Fonctions de la parenthèse dans *Nadja* d'André Breton." In *Recherches en science des textes*, ed. Yves Gohin. Grenoble: Presses Universitaires Grenoble, 1977, 181–88.

Goldyka, Jadwiga. "André Breton, romancier ou prosateur." *Romanica Wratislaviensia*, 416 (1979), 61–80.

Gollut, Jean-Daniel. "'Arcane 17.'" In *Le Surréalisme dans le texte*, ed. Daniel Bougnoux. Grenoble: Pubs. de l'Univ. des Langues & Lettres de Grenoble, 1978, 297–307.

Gratton, J. "Runaway: Textual Dynamics in the Surrealist Poetry of André Breton." *Forum for Modern Language Studies*, 18, no. 2 (1982), 126–41.

Guedj, Colette. *"Nadja* d'André Breton, ou l'exaltation réciproque du texte et de la photographie." *Les Mots, La Vie,* numéro hors série (1984), 91–136.

Guiette, Robert. "L'Amateur d'anthologies." *Bulletin de l'Académie Royale de langue et de littérature françaises,* 51 (1973), 119–24.

Guillaumin, Jean. "Rêve, réalité et surréalité dans la cure psychanalytique et ailleurs: rêve et poésie, avec une étude sur un rêve d'André Breton." In his *Le Rêve et le moi.* Paris: Presses universitaires de France, 1979.

Halpern, Joseph. "Breton's Overheated Room." *French Forum,* 7, no. 1 (1982), 46–57.

Heistein, Josef. "La Pensée littéraire de l'avant-garde. Du Futurisme au premier Manifeste de Breton." *Beiträge zur Romanischen Philologie,* 1 (1977), 70–82.

Helm, Michael. "Surrealismen, marxismen og den indre erfaring." *Vindrosen,* 20, no. 3, 2–12.

Henein, Georges. "Avec André Breton." *Grid,* 5 (Winter 1986–87), 42.

Hubert, Renée Riese. "The Artbook as Poetic Code: Breton's *Yves Tanguy." L'Esprit Créateur,* 22, no. 4 (1982), 56–66.

———. *"Nadja* depuis la mort de Breton (fiches signalétiques)." *Oeuvres et Critiques,* 2, no. 1 (1977), 93–102.

Jaguer, Edouard. "André Breton: Changer la vie – Changer la vue." *L'Orne littéraire,* 10 (1987), 32–44.

———. "Cambiare la vita, cambiare la vista/Changer la vie, changer la vue." *Terzoocchio,* 30 (March 1984), 11–15.

Janover, Louis. "Breton/Blum: brève rencontre qui en dit long (du temps que les surréalistes étaient marxistes." *Mélusine,* 8 (1986), 91–110.

Jean, Denis-J. "An Invitation Refused: André Breton and Surrealism in England in 1959." *Dada/Surrealism,* 5 (1975), 77–79.

Jones, Luisa. *"Nadja* and the Language of Poetic Fiction." *Dada/Surrealism,* 3 (1973), 45–52.

Kalandra, Záviš "L'Acte d'André Breton." *Change,* 25 (1975), 58–60.

Kapidžić-Osmanagić, Hanifa. "André Breton ili žudnja za totalnošću." *Izraz,* 22 (1978), 1269–1308.

Kirsch, Vicki. "Ghost-Ridden Authors/Ghost-Written Texts: Female Phantoms in Two Works by André Breton and Georges Bataille." *Paroles Gelées* (Los Angeles), 5 (1987), 37–53.

Knowlton, Edgar C., Jr. "Breton's 'Rano Raraku.' " *Explicator,* 40, no. 4 (1982), 50–52.

Kochmann, René. "Une maison peu solide: lecture d'un texte de Breton." *Australian Journal of French Studies,* 21, no. 1 (1984), 85–109.

Kritzman, Lawrence D. "For a Structural Analysis of *Nadja:* A Scientific Experiment." *Rackham Literary Studies,* 4 (1973), 9–23.

Kroymann, Maren. " 'Déchiffrer la femme.' Eine Lektüre von Bretons *Nadja." Lendemains,* 25–26 (1982), 168–76.

Ladimer, Bethany. "Madness and the Irrational in the Work of André Breton: A Feminist Perspective." *Feminist Studies,* 6 (1980), 175–79.

Laffitte, Maryse. "De l'atopie à l'utopie: Petit dialogue entre Baudelaire et Breton." *Revue Romane,* 18, no. 1 (1983), 61–72.

139

————. "L'Image de la femme chez Breton: Contradictions et virtualités." *Revue Romane*, 11 (1976), 286–305.

Lamba, Jacqueline. "Entretien avec Arturo Schwarz sur la rencontre Trotsky-Breton." *Lettres Nouvelles* (Sept.–Oct. 1975), 99–111.

Lamy, Suzanne. "Breton-Duras. B.D. Ma bande dessinée ou lecture d'une confluence." *Mélusine*, 4 (1983), 111–22.

————. "Le lexique 'traditionel' d' *Arcane 17*." *Mélusine*, no. 2 (1981), 152–74.

Lapachérie, Jean-Charles. "Breton critique d'Apollinaire: le calligramme comme bégaiement." *Que vlo-ve?* (April–June 1985), 16–20.

Lapachérie, Jean-Gérard. "Un 'topos' de la pensée du XVIIIe siècle dans les textes 'théoriques' d'André Breton." *Mélusine*, 7 (1985), 219–24.

Lebel, Robert. "André Breton: initiateur de la peinture surréaliste." In José Pierre, *L'Aventure surréaliste autour d'André Breton* [exhibition catalog]. Paris: Filipacchi, 1986.

————. "De Dada au surréalisme." *XXe Siècle*, 36, no. 42 (June 1974), 74–80.

————. "Marcel Duchamp and André Breton." In *Marcel Duchamp*, ed. Anne d'Harnoncourt and Kynaston McShine. New York: Museum of Modern Art, 1973.

Legrand, Gérard. "Un non-anti-philosophe." In *André Breton ou le surréalisme, même*, ed. Marc Saporta. Lausanne: L'Age d'Homme, 1988, 182–92.

Lehouck, E. "La Lecture surréaliste de Charles Fourier." *Australian Journal of French Studies*, 20, no. 1 (1983), 26–36.

Leroy, Claude. "L'Amour fou, même," *Revue des Sciences Humaines*, 4, no. 184 (1981), 119–24.

Leuwers, Daniel. "Jouve, Breton et la psychanalyse." *La Nouvelle Revue Française* (1 December 1979), 100–106.

Levy, Karen. "André Breton and the Artist's Gesture." In *Studies in Language and Literature*. Ed. Charles Nelson. Richmond: Dept. of Foreign Langs., Eastern Kentucky University, 1976, 337–41.

Levy, Sidney. "André Breton's *Nadja* and 'Automatic Writing.' " *Dada/Surrealism*, 2 (1972), 28–31.

Liberati, André. "Théorie et pratique de la poésie." In *André Breton ou le surréalisme, même*, ed. Marc Saporta. Lausanne: L'Age d'Homme, 1988, 49–55.

Lienhard, Pierre-André. "De Nadja à Mélusine: le génie féminin de la médiation." In *La Femme et le Surréalisme*. Ed. Erika Billetter and José Pierre. Lausanne: Musée cantonal des Beaux-Arts, 1987, 64–73.

Lima, Maria Isabel Pires de. "Nadja entre Mélusine et Méduse." *Coloquio Letras* (Lisbon), 72 (March 1983), 41–50.

Lourau, René. "André Breton und die *Nouvelle Revue Française*." In *Surrealismus*, ed. Peter Bürger. Darmstadt: Wissenschaftliche Buchgesellschaft, 1982.

Magritte, René. "Sur la mort d'André Breton." In *Ecrits complets*, ed. André Blavier. Paris: Flammarion, 1979.

Manu, Emil. "André Breton – Tristan Tzara in culisele congresului avangardei de la Paris." *Manuscriptum*, 9, no. 1 (1979), 133–40.

Martin, Claude. *"Nadja* et le mieux-dire." *Revue d'Histoire Littéraire de la France*, 72, 274–86.

Mary, Georges. "Les deux convulsions de Nadja ou le livre soufflé." *Mélusine*, 3 (1982), 207–14.

———. "Mélusine, ou le lieu d'un change: La Dynamique des figures dans 'Arcane 17.'" *Poétique*, 15, no. 60 (1984), 489–98.

Matthews, J. H. "André Breton Already?" *Modern Language Quarterly*, 33 (September 1972), 327–34.

———. "André Breton and Joan Miro: *Constellations.*" *Symposium*, 34 (1980), 353–76.

———. "André Breton, Jacques Brunius, and Surrealism in England." *Dada/Surrealism*, 6 (1976), 5–9.

———. "Désir et merveilleux dans *Nadja* d'André Breton." *Symposium*, 27 (1973), 246–68.

———. " 'Le Désir qui ne se refuse rien': *Les Vases communicants* d'André Breton." *Symposium*, 31 (1977), 212–30.

———. "Grammar, Prosody and French Surrealist Poetry." *Dada/Surrealism*, 9 (1979), 83–97.

———. "The Language of Objects." In his *Languages of Surrealism*. Columbia, MO: University of Missouri Press, 1986, 177–94.

———. "Une Contrée ou le désir est roi': *L'Amour fou* d'André Breton." *Symposium*, 33 (1979), 25–40.

Mercier, A. "André Breton et l'ordre figuratif dans les années 20." In *Le Retour à l'ordre dans les arts plastiques et l'architecture 1919–1925*. Paris: Spadem, 1976, 277–316.

Metzidakis, Stamos. "Picking Up Narrative Pieces in a Surrealist Prose Poem." *Orbis Literarum: International Review of Literary Studies*, 40, no. 4 (1985), 317–26.

Morel, Jean-Pierre. "Aurelia, Gradiva, x: Psychanalyse et poésie dans *Les Vases communicants.*" *Revue de Littérature Comparée*, 46, 68–89.

Mourier-Casile, Pascaline. "Du pagure à l'agate." In *André Breton ou le surréalisme, même*, ed. Marc Saporta. Lausanne: L'Age d'Homme, 1988, 141–53.

———. "Mélusine ou la triple en phase; Fée, Lilith, Phé dans *Arcane 17.*" *Mélusine*, 2 (1981), 175–202.

Navarri, Roger. "*Nadja*, ou l'écriture malheureuse." *Europe*, 528, 186–95.

Novaković, Jelena. "Bretonova poetika imaginarnog." *Izraz* (Belgrade), 31 (July –August 1987), 120–40.

———. "Le Miroir du merveilleux de Breton." *Izraz* (Belgrade), 12 (1985), 623–67.

Nussbaum, Laureen. "Breton's *Nadja* and Aragon's *Le Paysan de Paris:* An Evaluation of Two Surrealist Non-Novels." *Proceedings of the Pacific Northwest Conference on Foreign Languages*, 26, no. 1 (1975), 92–97.

Orenstein, Gloria F. "*Nadja* Revisited: A Feminist Approach." *Dada/Surrealism*, 8 (1978), 91–106.

———. "Reclaiming the Great Mother: A Feminist Journey to Madness and Back in Search of a Goddess Heritage." *Symposium*, 36, no. 1 (1982), 45–70.

Oxenhandler, Neal. "Cocteau, Breton, and Ponge: The Situation of the Self." In *About French Poetry*. Ed. Mary Ann Caws. Detroit: Wayne State Univ. Press, 1974, 54–68.

Pabst, Walter. "André Breton: Saisons (Breton/Soupault: *Les Champs Magnétiques*, 2.)." In his *Die moderne französische Lyrik: Interpretationen.* Berlin: Schmidt, 1976, 140-60.

Palayret, Guy. "Attirances et répulsions: Aragon, Breton et les écrivains révolutionnaires autour du PCF (1930-1935)." *Mélusine*, 5 (1983), 79-100.

Parmentier, Michel A. "André Breton et la question de l'unité du psychisme." *Australian Journal of French Studies*, 20, no. 1 (1983), 50-60.

———. "La Visée thérapeutique du surréalisme." *Mosaic*, 15, no. 3 (1982), 63-77.

Passeron, René. "Une dialectique de la création." In *André Breton ou le surréalisme, même*, ed. Marc Saporta. Lausanne: L'Age d'Homme, 1988, 106-12.

Pastoureau, Henri. "André Breton, l'homme que j'ai connu." *L'Orne Littéraire*, 3 (January 1983).

———. "Fragments analytiques." In *André Breton ou le surréalisme, même*, ed. Marc Saporta. Lausanne: L'Age d'Homme, 1988, 17-32.

Pellat, J.-Christophe. "L'Emploi des temps dans un texte narratif: André Breton *L'Amour Fou* chapitre IV." *L'Information Grammaticale*, 34 (June 1987), 31-35.

Penning, Dieter. "Der Begriff der Ueberwirklichkeit: Nerval, Maupassant, Breton." In *Phantastik in Literatur und Kunst*, ed. C. W. Thomsen and J. M. Fischer. Darmstadt: Wissenschaftliche Buchgesellschaft, 1980.

Péret, Benjamin. "Portrait of André Breton" [poem]. *The Malahat Review*, 51 (July 1975), 54.

Periz, Didier. "Autour de *Légitime Défense.*" *Docsur*, 4 (October 1987), 1-4.

Pierre, José. "Ainsi est la beauté." In *André Breton ou le surréalisme, même*, ed. Marc Saporta. Lausanne: L'Age d'Homme, 1988, 125-34.

———. "André Breton et la peinture." *L'Information Littéraire*, 32, 68-71.

———. "André Breton et le poème-objet." In *L'Objet au défi.* Ed. J. Chénieux-Gendron and M.-C. Dumas. Paris: Presses universitaires de France, 1987, 131-42.

———. "André Breton et/ou *Minotaure.*" In *Regards sur 'Minotaure,' la revue à tête de bête.* Genèva: Skira, 1987.

Pillet, Alain-Pierre. "André Breton à Venise: le plaisir d'une enquête." In *Du surréalisme et du plaisir.* Ed. J. Chénieux-Gendron. Paris: José Corti, 1987, 251-60.

Plottel, Jeanine. "Surrealist Archives of Anxiety." *Yale French Studies*, 66 (1984), 121-36.

Plouvier, Paule. "De l'utilisation de la notion freudienne de sublimation par André Breton." *Pleine Marge*, 5 (June 1987), 41-51.

Porter, Laurence M. " 'L'Amour fou' and Individuation: A Jungian Reading of Breton's *Nadja.*" *L'Esprit Créateur*, 22, no. 2 (1982), 25-34.

Pouget, Christine. "L'Attrait de la parapsychologie ou la tentation expérimentale." *Mélusine*, 2 (1981), 70-97.

———. "La Séduction de l'irrationnel." In *André Breton ou le surréalisme, même*, ed. Marc Saporta. Lausanne: L'Age d'Homme, 1988, 163-71.

Prince, Gerald. "La Fonction méta-narrative dans *Nadja.*" *French Review*, 49 (1976), 342-46.

Py, Françoise. "Les Pigments et les mots." In *André Breton ou le surréalisme, même*, ed. Marc Saporta. Lausanne: L'Age d'Homme, 1988, 99-105.

Quérière, Yves de la. "Les Chaînes verbales de 'L'Union libre.' " *Teaching Language through Literature,* 24, no. 1 (1984), 11–25.

Qvarnström, Gunnar. "Surrealismen nanifesterar sig." *Lyrikvännen,* 4 (1973), 34–43.

Raillard, Georges. "Comment André Breton s'est approprié les constellations." *Opus International,* 58 (Feb. 1976), 52–60.

Reboul, Jacquette. "André Breton ou la quête du Graal." In her *Critique universitaire et critique créatice.* Paris: Aux Amateurs du Livre, 1986.

"Le 'Réseau Breton' et la chasse aux rouges." In *Documents relatifs à la fondation de l'Internationale situationniste,* ed. G. Berreby. Paris: Allia, 1985.

Richter, Mario. "*Nadja* d'André Breton: Analyse de la première séquence." *Zeitschrift für französische Sprache und Literatur,* 96, no. 3 (1986), 225–37.

Riffaterre, Michael. "Intertextualité surréaliste." *Mélusine,* 1 (1979), 27–37.

Rioux, G. "A propos des expositions internationales du surréalisme: un document de 1947 et quelques considérations." *Gazette des Beaux-Arts,* 120, no. 1311 (April 1978), 163–71.

Robert, Bernard-Paul. "A propos d'André Breton." *Revue de l'Université d'Ottawa,* 46 (1976), 128–44.

———. "Breton, Engels et le matérialisme dialectique." *Revue de l'Université d'Ottawa,* 46 (1976), 293–308.

———. "Surréalisme, métapsychique et psychiatrie classique." *Studi Francesi,* 63 (1977), 498–500.

Roche, Gérard. "Breton, Trotsky: une collaboration." *Pleine Marge,* 3 (May 1986), 73–94.

———. "Changer la vie, transformer le monde." In *André Breton ou le surréalisme, même,* ed. Marc Saporta. Lausanne: L'Age d'Homme, 1988, 172–81.

———. "La Rencontre de l'aigle et du lion. Trotsky, Breton et le manifeste de Mexico." *Cahiers Léon Trotsky,* 25 (March 1986), 23–46.

Rose, Alan. "For an Independent Revolutionary Art: André Breton's Manifesto with Leon Trotsky." *European Studies Journal,* 2, no. 1 (1985), 52–61.

Rosolato, Guy. "L'Amour fou." In *Du surréalisme et du plaisir.* Ed. J. Chénieux-Gendron. Paris: José Corti, 1987, 125–36.

———. "La Haine de la musique." In his *Psychanalyse et musique.* Paris: Les Belles Lettres, 1982, 153–55.

Rossani, W. "Posizione di André Breton." *Osservatore Politico Letterario* 18, no. 8, 65–74.

Saporta, Marc. "L'Episode américain." In *André Breton ou le surréalisme, même,* ed. Marc Saporta. Lausanne: L'Age d'Homme, 1988, 33–35.

Sarkany, Stéphane. "*Nadja* ou la lecture du monde objectif." *Mélusine,* 4 (1983), 101–9.

Schmelz, Gabriele. "Bretons 'Köstliche Leiche'– Notizen zu einem Schreibspiel." *Deutschunterricht,* 4 (1980), 98–101.

Schoenfeld, Jean Snitzer. "André Breton, Alchemist." *The French Review,* 57, no. 4 (1984), 493–502.

———. "André Breton and the Poet/Reader." *Dada/Surrealism,* 13 (1984), 115–22.

Schuster, Jean. "17 sans 13." In his *Les Fruits de la passion.* Paris: L'Instant, 1988, 9–29.

Schwarz, Arturo. "L'Amour est l'érotisme. De quelques correspondances entre la pensée surréaliste et celles de l'alchimie et du tantrisme." *Mélusine*, 4 (1983), 179-202.

Sheringham, Michael. "Breton and the Language of Automatism: Alterity, Allegory, Desire." *Forum for Modern Language Studies*, 18, no. 2 (1982), 142-58.

———. "From the Labyrinth of Language to the Language of the Senses: The Poetry of André Breton." In *Sensibility and Creation: Studies in Twentieth-Century French Poetry*. Ed. Roger Cardinal. New York: Barnes & Noble, 1977, 72-102.

———. "*Mont de piété* and André Breton's Early Poetic Development." *Forum for Modern Language Studies*, 15 (1979), 46-68.

———. "Rimbaud in 1875 and André Breton's 'Forêt-noire.' " *French Studies*, 35, no. 1 (1981), 32-44.

Simpkins, S. "Surrealism and Breton's 'Textes solubles': An Index to Modernism." *Comparative Literature Studies*, 25, no. 3 (1988), 242-50.

Somville, Léon. "Pour une théorie des débuts: Une Analyse de l'incipit de l'oeuvre d'André Breton." In *Surréalisme dans le texte*. Ed. Daniel Bourgnoux. Grenoble: Pubs. de l'Univ. des langues & lettres de Grenoble, 1978, 41-57.

Spada, Marcel. "Gustave Moreau et l'Eve nouvelle d'André Breton." In *Des Mots et des couleurs: études sur le rapport de la littérature et de la peinture*, ed. P. Bonnefis and P. Reboul. Lille: Publications de l'Université de Lille, 1979.

Stalloni, Yves. "Pour une lecture de *Nadja* comme introduction au surréalisme." *Ecole des Lettres*, no. 11 (1983), 3-16.

Stamelman, Richard. "André Breton and the Poetry of Intimate Presence." *Dada/Surrealism*, 5 (1975), 58-65.

Steel, David A. "Autour d'un poème de jeunesse d'André Breton: 'Pour Lafcadio.' " In *Théorie, tableau, texte*, ed. Mary Ann Caws. Paris: Lettres Modernes, 1978.

Steinmetz, Jean-Luc. "Le Surréalisme interdit." *Revue des Sciences Humaines*, 4, no. 184 (1981), 33-58.

Stoll, André. "Beatrice im Versteck: zu Bretons surrealistischer Revolution; *Nadja.*" *Merkur*, 38, no. 4 (1984), 380-91.

Suleiman, Susan R. "Nadja, Dora, Lol V. Stein: Women, Madness and Narrative." In *Discourse in Psychoanalysis and Literature*, ed. S. Rimmon-Kenan. London: Methuen, 1987.

Tabart, Claude-André. "André Breton: *Clair de terre.*" *Ecole des Lettres*, 11 (1983), 17-23.

———. "André Breton: 'Noeud des miroirs.' " *École des Lettres*, 10 (1985).

Tamuly, Annette. "André Breton et la notion d'équivoque." *Mélusine*, 5 (1983), 195-207.

Taracido, Susan L. "Breton: A Poetry of Sensual Union." *Publications of the Missouri Philological Association*, 7 (1982), 43-47.

Testud, Pierre. "*Nadja*, ou la métamorphose." *Revue des Sciences Humaines*, 144 (1971), 579-89.

Tran Van Khai, Michelle. "Flagrant hasard, déflagrations du plaisir." In *Du surréalisme et du plaisir*. Ed. J. Chénieux-Gendron. Paris: José Corti, 1987, 111-23.

Tremaine, Louis. "Breton's *Nadja*: A Spiritual Ethnography." *Studies in Twentieth Century Literature*, 1 (1976), 91-119.

144

Ungar, Steven. "Sartre, Breton, and Black Orpheus: Vicissitudes of Poetry and Politics." *L'Esprit Créateur,* 17 (1977), 3–18.

Velasquez, J. Ignacio. "Breton y su double sombre: Nadja." In *Litoral* (November 1987), 425–37.

Vermeersch, Pierre. "André Breton et la recherche du tychique dans *Les Vases communicants.*" *Psychologie médicale,* 14, no. 9 (1982), 1373–79.

Vincent, Mona. "André Bretons *Nadja:* Struktur-och Meningsanalys av en Surrealistik Roman." *Samlaren,* 102 (1981), 26–36.

Virmaux, Alain, and Odette Virmaux. "Le Cinéma: un autre 'bilan d'infortune.' " In *André Breton ou le surréalisme, même,* ed. Marc Saporta. Lausanne: L'Age d'Homme, 1988, 87–98.

Vogt, Ulrich. "Au lavoir noir, ou du mythique dans le texte surréaliste." In *L'Objet au défi.* Ed. J. Chénieux-Gendron and M.-C. Dumas. Paris: Presses universitaires de France, 1987, 21–37.

———. "Osiris anarchiste, le miroir noir du surréalisme." *Mélusine,* 5 (1983), 142–58.

Wagner, Nicholas. "*Nadja,* ville de l'angoisse." *Travaux de Linguistique et de Littérature publiés par le Centre de Philologie et de Littératures Romanes de l'Université de Strasbourg,* 19, no. 2 (1976), 221–28.

Waite, A. "Meaning and Absence in Breton's *Nadja.*" *Romanic Review,* 77, no. 4 (1986), 376–90.

Warehime, Marja. "Beginning and Ending: The Utility of Dreams in *Les Vases Communicants.*" *French Forum,* 6, no. 2 (1981), 163–71.

NOTES ON CONTRIBUTORS

MARTINE ANTLE teaches French at the University of Wisconsin-Madison. She is the author of *Théâtre et poésie surréalistes: Vitrac et la scène virtuelle* and is currently working on a book on De Chirico, Delvaux and Léonor Fini.

ANNA BALAKIAN taught French and Comparative Literature at New York University. Her publications include *The Literary Origins of Surrealism* (1947), *Surrealism: The Road to the Absolute* (1959), *André Breton: Magus of Surrealism* (1971), and studies on Baudelaire, Mallarmé, Apollinaire, Symbolism and post-symbolist poets.

MICHEL BEAUJOUR teaches French literature at New York University. He has written numerous essays on Surrealism and poetics. A translation of his *Miroirs d'encre* is forthcoming under the title *Literary Self-Portrayal*.

HENRI BÉHAR teaches French literature at the Sorbonne Nouvelle-Paris III. He is the director of the Centre de Recherche sur le Surréalisme, and editor of the annual publication *Mélusine*. His publications include *Le Théâtre dada et surréaliste* (1979), *Jarry dramaturge* (1980), *Le Surréalisme* (1984, with Michel Carassou), and *Les Pensées d'André Breton* (1988).

MARY ANN CAWS teaches French and Comparative Literature at the Graduate Center of the City University of New York. Her publications include *The Poetry of Dada and Surrealism* (1970), *André Breton* (1971), *The Eye in the Text* (1981), *Reading Frames in Modern Fiction* (1985), and *The Art of Interference* (1988).

JACQUELINE CHÉNIEUX-GENDRON is a member of the research team Champs des activités surréalistes. She is the editor of the journal *Pleine Marge,* and her publications include *Le Surréalisme et le roman* (1983), *Le Surréalisme* (1984), and *L'Objet au défi* (1987, with Marie-Claire Dumas).

MARGARET COHEN teaches Comparative Literature at New York University. She is currently working on Walter Benjamin's relation to Surrealism, and on feminism and the social novel.

RUDOLF KUENZLI teaches English and Comparative Literature and directs the International Dada Archive at the University of Iowa. He is the coauthor of *Dada Artifacts* (1978) and *Dada Spectrum: The Dialectics of Revolt* (1979), editor of *New York Dada* (1986), *Dada and Surrealist Film* (1987), and *Marcel Duchamp: Artist of the Century* (1989).

J. H. MATTHEWS taught French at Syracuse University until his recent sudden death. His publications include *André Breton* (1967), *Surrealism and Film* (1971), *Theatre in Dada and Surrealism* (1974), *Benjamin Péret* (1975), *Towards a Poetics of Surrealism* (1976), *The Imagery of Surrealism* (1977), *The Inner Dream: Céline as Novelist* (1978), *Surrealism and American Feature Films* (1979), *Eight Painters: The Surrealist Connection* (1982), *Surrealism, Insanity, and Poetry* (1982), *Joyce Mansour* (1985), *Languages of Surrealism* (1986), and *André Breton: Sketch for an Early Portrait* (1986).

JOSÉ PIERRE is a member of the research team Champs des activités surréalistes. His recent publications include *Surréalisme et anarchie* (1983), *L'Univers surréaliste* (1983), *L'Aventure surréaliste autour d'André Breton* (1986), and *André Breton et la peinture* (1987).

STAMOS METZIDAKIS teaches French literature at Washington University in St. Louis. He is the author of *Repetition and Semiotics: Interpreting Prose Poems* (1986), and is currently writing a book on the rise of literary pluralism.

MICHAEL RIFFATERRE is University Professor at Columbia University in New York. His publications include *Essais de stylistique structurale* (1971), *La Production du texte* (1979), and *Semiotics of Poetry* (1978).

RONNIE SCHARFMAN teaches French at the State University of New York at Purchase. She is the author of *Engagement and the Language of the Subject in the Poetry of Aimé Césaire,* and is currently preparing a book on exile and nomadism in E. Jabès.

JOHN ZUERN is a doctoral student in the Program in Comparative Literature at the University of Texas at Austin. He is currently writing his dissertation on autobiographical narratives.